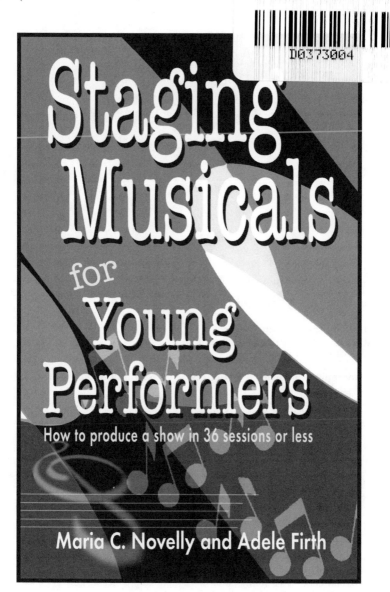

Staging Musicals
for Young Performers

How to produce a show in 36 sessions or less

Maria C. Novelly and Adele Firth

MERIWETHER PUBLISHING LTD.
Colorado Springs, Colorado

Meriwether Publishing Ltd., Publisher
PO Box 7710
Colorado Springs, CO 80933-7710

Editor: Arthur L. Zapel
Editorial Assistant: Dianne Bundt
Cover design: Jan Melvin

Photography: Photos courtesy of Maria Novelly and Adele Firth

© Copyright MMIV Meriwether Publishing Ltd.
Printed in the United States of America
First edition

Library of Congress Cataloging-in-Publication Data

Novelly, Maria C.
  Staging musicals for young performers : how to produce a show in 36 sessions or less / Maria C. Novelly & Adele Firth.--1st ed.
     p. cm.
  ISBN 1-56608-099-1
  1. Musicals--Production and direction. I. Firth, Adele. II. Title.
  MT955.N76 2004
  792.602'32--dc22

                              2004010189

        1   2   3   04   05   06

For Bill Lawson

For Matt and Amy

We would like to acknowledge the theatrical genius and continuing influence of Adele's father, Bill Lawson, whose name and vast knowledge of theatre lives on in the Adele Lawson School of Theatre. He leaves memories of a brilliant mind, a wonderful life, a remarkable man.

We would also like to honor the memory of Maria's high school drama teacher, Doris Hury, whose constant admonition of "We go first class!" set high standards worth achieving.

We would like to thank all the musicians we have worked with. Their abilities constantly amaze us, and their genius has frequently rescued a show from a tight spot.

Finally and most of all, we would like to pay tribute to all the young actors we have had the honor to work with. You have been an inspiration.

Contents

Introduction

Musicals have the advantage of providing a way to showcase a large number of performers. Musicals present opportunities for your entire group to perform using a range of skills — singing, movement, dance, and musical accompaniment, as well as acting.

If you don't yet have the experience or skills in directing all the aspects of a musical — that is, acting, singing, dance, movement, and technical production — this book will guide you in building your own skills or finding resources to help you.

Musicals have wide appeal to all ages. You will usually get a bigger crowd for a musical than you do for a straight play, and since your group works hard to prepare a show, don't they deserve the largest possible audience?

This book will help you in these situations:

- You are working with a group of kids at a school, church, or youth center, and they decide they want to put on a musical.
- You have decided you want to build a drama club that meets after school or on weekends, but aren't sure what to do and how to structure the sessions.
- You find yourself numbly saying, "I have just been told I have to do the school show. *What* am I going to do?"
- You have been directing musicals for some time, but are looking for some tips on rehearsal management and organizing the performers and parents.

This book aims to show you how you can stage almost any musical show on any budget, whether you are operating on a shoestring or producing a sponsored extravaganza. It provides information and guidance about all the things you *must* think about (such as fire regulations and insurance for your group) as well as the things you *want* to think about (such as characterization and costumes). If you are a newly appointed, inexperienced director, don't be discouraged by how many elements need to be considered. Just take it a step at a time, and concentrate on the kids having a good time at each session you run.

This book focuses on working with musical scripts, not "straight plays" (non-musical plays). However, many of the ideas and much of the advice presented in this book will be useful to both novice and experienced directors of straight plays.

This book assumes you are working with a group of about twenty-five to thirty-five performers, ages six to fifteen who have a range of commitment and talent. This book also assumes you will be working with your group for about two hours per week, over a ten-month period. The two-hour weekly sessions are organized into blocks of about six weeks, which corresponds to how the school year is organized in many local school districts in the U.S.A. or educational authorities in the U.K.

Based on our experience, you should expect to add a few extra sessions for technical and dress rehearsals just before the performance. You may also need to add a few extra hours to work with a small number of principals and soloists. All in all, the total number of rehearsal hours is about eighty to ninety. If your production plans include building and painting sets, you need to plan some extra sessions that only your "building crew" will attend.

If your schedule is structured differently, (for example, you have a drama class for a total of four hours per week or you meet after school for a three-hour session each week) you can use the total number of hours to calculate how many weeks or months you will need to produce your show. During summer vacation or school holidays, you can do a show in three weeks of solid rehearsal, all day, every day. This total immersion approach can be extremely successful because the children see the results of their efforts after only a few weeks. When you meet weekly, you must by necessity spend some time each week reviewing because most of your cast will not be thinking about the show except when they are at a rehearsal!

We believe that young performers — and their performances — are not helped by too tight a directorial control or endless rehearsal. Spending hours of extra time choreographing every gesture or dictating every vocal inflection may indeed produce a more "professional" production, but it will lack the energy and vitality of a show in which the performers are permitted to make as many of their own decisions — and occasional mistakes — as possible. Also, if you try to rehearse at this level of detail, it will be difficult to cover the entire script, and it is doubtful the actors will remember your instructions.

Chapter 1

Selecting Your Musical

In selecting a script, the first question is always the same: Can it be done? From this book's perspective, the answer is always "Yes!" because shows can be simplified to a level suitable to your group. The answer in your specific situation depends on availability of talent, license, and to a lesser degree, budget. This section helps you decide the answer. Don't feel overwhelmed by all the things you will need to consider and eventually pull together, especially if you are new to running a group or producing musicals. The learning curve is steep, but short.

Assuming you have a fairly large group — say between twenty-five and thirty-five children, ranging in ages from six to fifteen — it is helpful to focus on scripts that have plenty of chorus scenes, lots of child characters, and whose principal roles are accessible to young performers in terms of musicality and characterization. A list of scripts appropriate to your age group, many of which we have produced, is given in the section "Strong scripts," later in this chapter.

Your audience, composed mostly of friends and family of the cast, won't be too bothered by what production they see and may actually be relieved to see something somewhat new or unusual. If you are unsure about what play to perform, you can usually read through "perusal" copies on loan from different publishers. Talk to local schools or amateur groups, and investigate what musicals they have produced. Contact adult theatre groups — they can frequently give you ideas or suggest other children's theatre groups you can talk to about your choice of script.

In this book we will be giving frequent examples from commonly produced shows such as *Annie* and *Oliver* because we assume that most people have seen them, usually as films, and can easily identify most of the scenes and characters we discuss. If you are new to directing musical theatre, you may feel more confident trying a script you have already seen yourself, if only the movie version. However, don't feel bound to producing only famous musicals. We also give examples from lively, large-cast musicals such as *Phantom of the Op'ry* and *Is There a Doctor in the House?*

Before you decide on any script, make sure it is actually available for performance and review its licensing costs against your budget.

Availability of License

You are legally required to have a license to perform other people's work, including musicals. Every script has a license holder for performance, which is usually a musical publisher (such as Music Theatre International (MTI) in the U.S.A, or Josef Weinberger in the U.K.), or a specialist drama publisher (such as Contemporary Drama Service, a division of Meriwether Publishing Ltd.). Lists of license holders can be found in Appendix 2 — Resources.

Depending on the specific musical, the license may or may not be available to you, so before you announce to your group that you are going to put on a particular show, check!. Some musicals are available only for professional performance. There may also be restrictions as to the country in which the play can be performed, so take care when reading those international websites!

Some license holders have developed "junior" or "school" editions of musicals. These versions usually omit salty language, racy scenes, and difficult musical numbers. For example, the junior version of *Guys and Dolls* cuts the strip number "Take Back Your Mink" and the song "Havannah." Junior versions may also offer you the option of purchasing kits to help plan the entire performance. However, junior or school versions often restrict the maximum age of the performers to twelve or fourteen, so check with the publisher before you decide on a show, especially if you are working with teenagers.

Strong scripts

Good scripts with large casts and roles suitable for children include:

Annie Get Your Gun
*Annie**
*Beauty and the Beast ***
Bugsy Malone
*Cool Suit ***
*Fiddler on the Roof **
*Guys and Dolls **
*Into the Woods **
*Is There a Doctor in the House?***
Joseph and the Amazing Technicolor Dreamcoat
*Les Misérables **
Oliver
*Once on This Island **
*Phantom of the Op'ry ***
*Schoolhouse Rock **
Scrooge
The Boyfriend
*Whistle Down the Wind**

West Side Story and *Grease* are ideal for groups that are mostly teenagers, although *Grease* is often unavailable, and both the music and dance in *West Side Story* are challenging.

*Junior or school editions have been advertised as available for these.
**No-royalty or nominal royalty large-cast scripts available from specialist drama publisher
  Contemporary Drama Service, a division of Meriwether Publishing Ltd.

Budget

It is possible to stage an enjoyable musical, whether you are working on the tiniest of budgets or with buckets of money. You can spend as much or as little as you like, make the show technically as complex or as simple as you prefer. The music, the lyrics, the dialog, the pathos, the comedy, and ultimately the energy of the performance are the heart and life of a musical. Scenery, lighting, costumes, and special effects are secondary.

Inspiring comments aside, you do need a fairly precise idea of how much your vision of the show will cost. This will then give you an idea of how much money you must commit yourself to raising if you don't already have such sums on hand. Your main costs will be licensing fees and/or royalties, which are determined by the license holder; additional help for the show, which depends on the show and how comfortable you are taking on certain roles and the cost of additional help; and production costs, over which you have quite a bit of control.

Licensing fees and royalty costs

To perform a script, you must pay a license fee to the license holder. In addition, some license holders also charge royalties, which are a percentage of your ticket revenue. The terms "royalty" and "license fee" are used interchangeably by some publishers.

The "adult" versions of widely known musicals such as *Guys and Dolls* and *Annie* command fees commensurate with their durability of appeal. However, junior or school versions of these same scripts charge smaller fees. If you are on a very tight budget, look at royalty-free musicals that require a one-time license fee and/or payment for a requisite number of scripts.

Directorial help you may need for certain shows

For musicals, you need to oversee musical and dance direction as well as the stage direction of a straight play. You may want to do all three roles yourself, but often there is a musical director responsible for the singing and musical accompaniment, and sometimes a separate choreographer. If you decide to mount a complex technical production, you may also need a separate technical director or designer.

You need to decide which roles you are willing to take on yourself and to whom you can delegate the others before you can answer the question, "Can I do this show?"

Musical director

Because a musical includes singing and often live music, it can be difficult to be both the acting director and the musical director. If you are the drama teacher at a school, the music teacher may be drafted to be the musical director. If you are running a private group, you will most likely need to find someone to be your musical director, and they will most likely charge a fee. For more information about what a musical director does, see the section "Singing" in chapter 10.

Choreographer

This book describes in detail how to build up a dance sequence and teach the steps. However, you may want a separate choreographer to work with your group, and again, that individual may charge a fee. See the section, "Choreography" in chapter 10 for more information about this role.

Technical director

The technical director is responsible for designing and integrating the set, lighting, and sound into the show. Sometimes the technical director may also have overall responsibility for costumes and makeup as well. If you are planning an elaborate production, you may need someone to oversee all the technical aspects of the show.

Production and other running costs

For now, your goal is to estimate what costs you will need to cover and to determine how they will be met. Details on the technical production, that is, lighting, sound, costumes, scenery, and properties are discussed in chapters 10 and 11. If you have little experience putting together a show, you may find it helpful to read these chapters now, before you work out your costs. Production costs include costs for the following.

Insurance and venue performance license

You will need liability insurance to cover your performers and audience members during the workshop sessions and performances. You may also need a "performance license" for the venue itself — a document that verifies that the building has adequate fire exits and other facilities for the size of audience you plan to entertain. For further information, see the sections "Insurance" and "Performance License" in chapter 2.

Performance and rehearsal venues

If you are working with a drama class, school drama club, church, or youth center group, you probably have appropriate space available, even though you may need to compete with other activities for its use. If you are operating privately, you need to allow for the costs of renting places for rehearsal and/or performance. For further information, see the section, "Venues for Rehearsal and Production" in chapter 2.

Lighting

Check to ensure that the performance hall has adequate lighting for the stage area. In our experience having *enough* light is more important than providing special lighting effects. So if you have only fluorescent tube lighting and no moveable spotlights or banks of colored lights, it won't stop the audience from enjoying themselves. However, they do get restless and distracted if they cannot see. Try out the lighting at the venue you are using and make provisions to add more if required. And unless you are prepared to pay for rewiring, check that your lighting plans don't outstrip the electrical capacity of the hall you intend to use! See chapter 12 for more information on lighting.

Costumes and makeup

Costumes can be essential to establishing character for the actor and the audience alike. If you do not already have access to a stock of costumes, you need to plan how you will costume the show and how much that will cost. You can usually get by with asking the cast members to provide the bulk of the costumes themselves and then rent the more unusual or extravagant outfits.

Traditional stage makeup is not really necessary for most characters. If you do decide to use makeup, determine what you are going to use and plan for the cost. See chapter 11 for more on costumes and makeup.

Scenery and properties ("props")

You can get away with using whatever standard curtains, tables, and chairs are already in the performance venue. However, if you have the money to spend, actors and audiences alike enjoy painted backdrops, stage scenery, and appropriate furniture. We provide ideas for a "minimalist" approach to a stage setting. Decide what you would like to have and estimate its cost.

Stage properties, or "props," refer to items used on stage. Props are occasionally essential to move the plot forward (for example, the locket in *Annie* or the books in *Oliver*) and they help portray character. For budgeting purposes, check the list of props that usually comes with the script, or go through the script and see if there is anything that may be expensive to buy or rent if you are unable to borrow it from someone for free. See chapter 11 for further details on scenery and props.

Sound equipment

You need to decide whether you will use microphones for the performers, which can be helpful during solo and duet songs. If you are playing music on a tape or CD during the performance, ensure that the stereo player and speakers you plan to use are adequate for the hall in which you will perform. If you are using any electronic instruments, such as a keyboard for musical accompaniment, check that the amplifier and speakers are substantial enough for the size of the performance hall. Check that the power supply is sufficient and whether you need to provide extra extension cables. Estimate costs accordingly. See chapter 12 for more information.

Live musical accompaniment

If you can possibly manage it, we recommend the use of live accompaniment. Young performers can sometimes struggle to keep pace with an accompaniment track, and live music adds texture to the show. Piano or keyboard and percussion are usually sufficient.

If you plan to use live music during the performance, the licensing fee charged by the publisher may vary according to the size of your band. Alternatively, the license may specify how many instruments you must have. You are not allowed to re-score the music yourself or alter it in any way. For budget-planning purposes, check the cost and availability of musicians and musical instruments you plan to use for both the rehearsals and the show. See the section "Equipment for Live or Recorded Musical Accompaniment" in chapter 12.

Recorded musical accompaniment

If you are performing a junior edition of a musical, the publisher may provide a tape or CD of the instrumental accompaniment to the songs in the show.

If you plan to use a commercially produced tape or CD during the performance as accompaniment or background music, you may need to pay a fee for performance rights. Assuming you already have the license to perform the show, the publisher may allow you to use, without paying additional fees, a recording that you make yourself of someone playing the music. Obviously, this recording should not be a recording of another production, but of a group of musicians you assemble for the specific purpose of producing an accompaniment tape for your show. Check with the specific publisher.

Promotion, tickets, and programs

The most effective and least costly promotion for any amateur show is cast members personally inviting people to come. However, you can help your cast provide information about the show by arming them with simple black and white flyers or posters to take home to their family and friends. You may also want to print more elaborate flyers, advertise in local papers, or try to get press coverage. Decide what promotion you would like to have and determine the costs.

Tickets usually need to be produced, and the audience and actors like to see a program for the show. Estimate the costs of producing these, which can be low or high, and can sometimes be met by advertising or sponsorship, assuming you have the time to pursue it. See chapter 13 on how to build an audience for your show.

Backstage and front-of-house help

Although we recommend you use the cast to move scenery and props backstage, you do need extra people to run the lights, produce off-stage sound effects, follow the prompt book, collect tickets, and sell refreshments. You can usually recruit these people from the parents, friends, and siblings of the company. See the section, "Strategies for Harnessing the Parental Workforce" in chapter 2.

On-stage Talent

In addition to estimating your required budget and checking that a script is available, you must also feel confident that your group can successfully perform the play in terms of acting, singing, and movement. Hopefully, upon reading this book, you will feel reasonably comfortable that you can take charge over all of the acting, musical, and dance direction, even though you may prefer that another adult be responsible for certain aspects of the production, such as musical direction. The purpose of this book is to help you develop skills in leading your performers to present the best show possible. At the same time, you must feel certain that your cast has enough raw talent that can be shaped into an enjoyable, satisfying performance.

Performance capability

If you are to mount a major production and invite a (usually) paying audience, you must find people in your group who can perform the major roles. If your group or class is new, you may wish to extend the audition period and delay announcing the show title so you have plenty of time to judge their potential to perform — possibly — any one of several scripts. Once your group gets going, the match between your talent pool and the demands of the script is easier to determine because you know the strengths and weaknesses of each member.

In musicals, singing talent is of paramount importance; it is dreadful indeed for the audience to sit through mangled song after mangled song. Singing talent means more than an ability to carry a tune; the actor must also be loud enough to be heard, sing with expression, and stay "in character." However, there are ways of helping match the singing talent with the role and of accommodating less than perfect voices. See chapter 7, "Casting the Show."

Acting talent involves more than just "feeling the part." Your actors must have the ability to memorize lines, pay attention on stage, and project their voices in the hall in which you will perform. In addition, particularly if they are young and inexperienced, they cannot become so nervous or feel so embarrassed in front of their peers that they "chicken out."

You can choreograph dances to keep movements as simple and straightforward as possible, but anyone who is a principal performer in a dance scene needs a good, natural sense of movement, and ideally, some dance training.

Gender issues

You may find that many scripts seem to hand their best leading and secondary roles to males. Your group, in contrast, may be 80 percent female. Compounding this challenge, the rules governing

13

most licenses for performance normally do *not* allow a character to change his or her gender. In other words, Auntie Mame cannot become Uncle Mark, and Oliver cannot become Olivia. However, actresses can pretend to be boys; for example, Eleanor can play Oliver.

If you are working with an all-girl or all-boy group and have no source of actors of the opposite sex, the answer is simple: you simply cast the entire show with whatever gender you are working with. Many all-boys schools present rousing Gilbert and Sullivan operettas with Mabel played by Michael and Angelina played by a falsetto-singing Alan.

A female Daddy Warbucks!

However, if you are working with a mixed group, you may often have more girls than boys, and, in some cases, you may have better actresses than you do actors. You have to decide how far you will take the audience in its "willing suspension of disbelief." Strictly speaking, if men played all roles in the time of Shakespeare, it shouldn't matter too much who plays whom in the twenty-first century.

If there are boys in the cast, it may be counter-intuitive for the audience to watch the romantic male lead played by a girl, but if your actress is strong enough, it can be achieved. At the very least, look carefully at the script and find as many characters as possible that could be quite believably played by girls. Some characters, although often played by men in mainstream or film productions, are in fact neutral and can be played by girls. Characters such as police officers, detectives, magicians, criminals, doctors, ministers, and even relations such as fathers or uncles can usually all be taken on by girls quite successfully, without changing them to policewomen, mothers, or aunts — particularly with six to eleven-year-olds. For example, in *Is There a Doctor in the House?*, Widow Stockade needs to be played as a female but could be acted by a male or a female, whereas the Preacher could be played as a female or as a male as the gender isn't mentioned. The role of Tom Sawyer Huckleberry Finn Jones, Jr., has to be played as male, but the role itself could be acted by a male or female.

Challenges presented by large groups

If you have a large number of young performers attending your Saturday workshop or after-school club, congratulations! However, you may face a challenge: you have more performers than some scripts actually call for. However, if you are to run a successful workshop, there's little point in having four stars permanently on-stage and thirty restless children off-stage.

Keep in mind that there is really no limit to the number of performers in certain types of scenes. There is no reason why there must be only seven orphans in *Annie* or twelve in *Oliver* — have twenty! Why limit yourself to five gamblers in *Guys and Dolls* — all spare performers can be gamblers *and* they can be members of the Salvation Army band in the next scene.

Even in shows written for large companies, such as *Is There a Doctor in the House?*, you can increase the number of roles, especially in dance numbers. For example, Pupils 1, 2, and 3 — with toothache, stomachache, and a headache — could easily be doubled by adding Pupil 4 (with an earache), Pupil 5 (with backache), Pupil 6 (with heartache), and so on. Alternatively, just have extra pupils with no named ailments and they can join in with the number "Pills, Pills!" As always, do check your licensing arrangements, but usually there is no restriction on the number of performers in dance scenes, or even roles being divided between several actors.

One of your most important goals is to get as many performers acting, singing, and dancing in as many scenes as possible. Another goal is to make each cast member a "star" for at least one wonderful moment in the show. See the section, "Casting each performer as a star" in chapter 7. Group members who feel they have nothing special to do or wind up sitting around a lot each session don't develop their skills very quickly, are likely to become bored and may drop out. Finally, most of your audience members have come to see someone they know in the show — so that someone needs to be seen as much as possible.

Chapter 2
Preparing to Run the Sessions

Liability Insurance

You will need public liability insurance for the kids who attend your workshops. If you are working as the school drama teacher, after-school drama coach, the church group leader, or the local scoutmaster, your organization's insurance will normally cover any accidents or injuries that might occur during your workshop sessions. Do check if you have any concerns. However, if you are running a private group, you need to arrange for liability insurance for your workshop to cover accident or injury at any venue in which you rehearse or perform. If you are renting a venue, the rental may include insurance; check the contract details.

You may also need insurance that protects against an audience member getting hurt while watching the show. If you do not have a crystal clear idea of your insurance coverage, check with the institution you are working with, or with the manager of the venue you plan to rent *before* you begin your sessions. For information about obtaining insurance, see Appendix 2 — Resources.

Child Worker Clearance (U.K.)

Parents, especially those with younger children, need to feel confident that you will work with the children in an entirely appropriate way. If you are running a private group in the U.K., you and the members of your team may have to or want to apply for a Criminal Record Bureau (CRB) Disclosure, which will help reassure parents that your background is suitable for working with children. If you are already working as a teacher, you are likely to

16

have already obtained a CRB Disclosure.

For information regarding any required or voluntary clearances needed to work with children in the U.S.A., please check with your state government authorities; in other countries, check with your local government authorities.

Venues for Rehearsal and Production

If you are a drama teacher in a school, you may have a hall, a cafeteria with a stage at one end, or a drama studio available for the performances, along with a classroom in which to run workshops and early rehearsals. If these areas are for shared use, you simply must make sure you reserve the space well in advance so you are not confronted with the gymnastics team when you show up for your final dress rehearsal.

If you are planning to run private sessions, you will need to secure venues for your workshop sessions and for the performances. It is handy to have the workshops, rehearsals, and performances take place in the same space, but it isn't necessary and it often isn't possible.

Where to seek venues

If you are without a rehearsal venue, start by asking everyone you know whether they know of any appropriate space. Almost every organization with property is under pressure to make sure it is fully utilized, and if space is available, you can usually rent it. Checking with the following organizations may help you find a space:

- Schools – They may have a hall, cafeteria, or auditorium you can use.
- Churches – They may have meeting rooms or halls available.
- Community centers – They often have meeting rooms and other facilities.
- Leisure clubs and other clubs – They may have rooms available.

In addition to approaching each possible venue separately, check to see if the local school district or other government authority (metropolitan or county councils in the U.K.) has a "lettings department" that will help you find available space.

Once you have come up with a few options, visit them and decide which will suit your needs the best.

17

Considerations if rehearsal and performance venues are separate

There are several advantages to holding rehearsals and performances in at least the same venue if not in the exact same room. The actors are familiar with the surroundings and the stage. Even if they don't move to the actual stage from a rehearsal room until the technical rehearsal, they can at least visit and walk around it beforehand. If you are lucky enough to hold a number of rehearsals on the actual stage, the actors will be working in the actual space they will be performing in, so they will know exactly where to move and how long movements will take. The performers will know where the props and costumes are stored. Finally, the parents know where the building is and how long it takes to get to it.

There are also advantages to having different venues for performance and rehearsal. Renting a large, performance-worthy theatre every week for thiry-six weeks can be an extremely costly, if not an unavailable, option. Renting a single, low-cost hall for workshops and performances may keep expenses down and provide continuity to your group, but that same hall may lack the theatrical facilities you would like to have during the actual shows. Separate venues may be the best option. Even if your rehearsal and performance venues do end up being miles apart, or if you are confined to a small classroom until just before the show, do not despair. We will give you hints and tips on making the smoothest possible transition from rehearsal space to stage; see the section "Making the transition from rehearsal to performance venue" in chapter 14.

In all cases, be sure to visit the venues before booking them, and double check that they will be available for the dates you require. Don't assume that if you used a particular venue last May, it will also be available this May. There's nothing like trying to find an alternative performance venue three weeks before the show opens to increase what are already fairly high levels of adrenaline.

Things to look for in a performance venue

In addition to costs, keep the following considerations in mind as you search out a performance venue.

Staging considerations

Your performance venue obviously needs a stage area and an audience area. Your stage area might be a raised stage with space for seating in front of it. It could also be a ground-level area with seating rising away from it. Unless you plan to use only two or three rows of seats, try to avoid using a stage area that is the same level as the audience. You will end up with a very frustrated group of theatergoers.

Other considerations of the venue as a performance area are:

Availability – Is it available, at the least, for a technical rehearsal and a dress rehearsal as well as the performance dates? The first performance should not be the first time the kids are on the stage.

Stage size – Try to visualize it filled with thirty performers and scenery. Is there enough room? Will the effect be crowded?

Floor – The floor where the actors will dance should be a safe, ideally sprung wooden floor, not concrete.

Curtains – If the stage is a classic proscenium stage with a frame-like opening to the performance area and curtains across it, check that the curtains work. Can they be drawn fully apart and pulled fully back together? If there is a back curtain, can it be completely drawn so a backdrop or cyclorama, if used, can be hung? Do the curtains meet current fire regulations? If the stage area has no curtains at all, where will the actors enter and exit? If there are curtains on the windows, will they block out the light adequately? Summer evenings can be quite light, or you may be planning matinees.

Provision of platforms or rostrums – Are any available for use at the venue? Will they be available the dates of the final rehearsals and performances?

Off-stage areas – With a curtained, proscenium stage, is there enough wing space — that is, the areas to the right, left, and behind the performance area — to accommodate the scenery, props, actors, costumes?

Dressing/waiting areas ("greenroom") – The actors must have somewhere to go when they are not on-stage. It is impossible for youngsters to remain silent in the wings for more than about ten seconds. Where can the actors go when they are not on-stage?

Secure storage areas – Is there storage space for your props, lights, scenery, and costumes between dress rehearsals and performances? Can things be left at the venue securely?

Piano – If you plan to use live music but don't have access to a full-scale band or orchestra, you will probably need a piano. Check if the venue has one, and check that it works and is in tune. Find out the whereabouts of the key if there is one. Check that the piano will still be there when you put on the performance and that the venue management doesn't have an inconvenient plan to sell it. If there is no piano, arrange to borrow or rent a keyboard and amplifier.

Lighting – If lighting equipment is provided, is a technician available to run it? If you are expected to work the lights yourself, where are the controls? Do they work? If you are expected to rig or change the lighting yourself, are adequate ladders and other equipment available?

Sound/PA equipment – If provided, is a technician available to run it? If you are expected to run it yourself, make sure the controls work and the speakers are adequate.

Electrical power supply – If you plan to bring in your own lighting, sound, or music equipment, is there enough power in the facility? Are there enough electrical outlets in the right places?

Insurance – Does the venue rent cover accidents or injuries that might happen to members of your group or the audience?

Trash cans/rubbish bins – Are there enough in the backstage and audience areas? You may be expected to take away all your litter each time you use the venue. If there aren't enough adequate receptacles, you may need to provide some — and some bin liners — for the audience and for your performers backstage during the performances.

Audience considerations

Venue performance license – Does the venue have a license, verifying that it meets building code requirements, such as fire exits, for an audience the size you plan to have? See section below, "Venue Performance License," for more details.

Location – Is it near to the rehearsal venue? Will parents and audience find it easily? A distant venue may put off your audience.

Seating – Are there enough chairs? Are they clean and in good condition? Test out the chairs, even if they are fixed. If the venue provides moveable chairs, find out how many are available. Test a few and make sure they are in good condition. Double check that the chairs will be available on the dates you require and aren't going to be moved into another room for the annual Church Council meeting that just happens to coincide with your opening night.

Restroom facilities – Consider the anticipated size of your audience and decide if these facilities are adequate.

Disabled access – Is there a ramp or other access for audience members who might be mobility-impaired? Are there suitable places for wheelchairs in the audience area?

Extra furniture – Are there extra tables or chairs that can be set out for refreshment sales or ticket sales?

Kitchen/refreshment facilities – If you plan to sell hot coffee or cold drinks before the show and during the intermission, are there facilities to heat water or to keep items cold?

Parking – Is there adequate parking at the venue or nearby for the size of audience you anticipate?

Things to look for in a rehearsal venue

Along with costs, keep the following considerations in mind when you look for a rehearsal/workshop venue:

Availability – The venue must consistently be available when you need it, which is usually outside school hours, for example, every Tuesday from 4 to 6 P.M. or every Saturday from 2 to 4 P.M. Your group and their parents will expect and appreciate consistency, as they usually have many other activities in their schedules and they dislike changes.

Normal activities in neighboring rooms – If you run your workshops next to the room where the regular bingo game, PTA meeting, or yoga class takes place, expect trouble. Your group will be excited, boisterous, and impossible to rein in, and you don't need the extra pressure of fruitlessly trying to keep them quiet.

Location – Is the location convenient for your potential workshop group and their parents? Is it easy for kids to be dropped off and picked up safely? What is the impact of rush-hour traffic, say, if you are running sessions from 4 to 6 P.M.?

Size – Is the room large enough to accommodate your cast as they work on numbers for the show? Is there room for you and others to watch the rehearsal and see the total picture?

Ventilation and room height – Your actors will be working hard and need to stay cool. Low ceilings usually mean a warm room. Find out what control you will have over ventilation, air conditioning (if available), and heating.

Type of floor – A concrete floor will wreak havoc on the knees of your performers when they dance. Ideally, your venue will have a sprung wooden floor where the actors will be practicing their dance movements.

Cleanliness – The floor area should be clean enough to sit down on. Does the space feel dusty? Dust causes problems for asthmatic children and makes singing and other vocal work difficult.

Piano – If you plan to use a piano for the performance, having one at the rehearsal venue is very helpful, particularly as you near the show dates. If one is available, see if it works properly and if it will be available every week. If there is no piano available, you may need to bring in a keyboard when necessary.

Electric sockets – As a minimum, you will need electricity for your portable stereo almost every week, and for the video player if you plan to show a video of the performance. You may also need electricity for a keyboard.

Furniture – Are tables and chairs available to be used during rehearsals?

Restroom/facilities – Check that they are available and clean.

Telephone – Despite the prevalence of cellular phones, it is helpful to have a phone available for emergencies.

Drinking water – See if a kitchen with drinking water or a water fountain is available. If not, instruct the participants to bring bottles of water (not carbonated drinks) to each session.

Storage areas – Is there any storage area available, particularly as performance time nears and you start working with props and scenery? How secure is it? It is very unusual for storage areas to be available, so you may have to bring props, costumes, and set pieces in for each session and remove them afterward.

Trash cans and removal – Check that there are adequate trash cans — they are sometimes inexplicably but completely missing. Inexpensive, high-usage rented facilities such as church halls or community centers may expect you to take all trash and rubbish with you when you leave, or at least take it to the dumpster, because they simply do not have the personnel onsite to provide ongoing cleaning services.

Venue Performance License

If you are using a public building, such as a town or church hall, please note the building itself must have a performance license for staging performances there. This is different from your license from the copyright holder, which is to perform a particular show.

A performance license for a venue is required to ensure that regulations regarding fire exits and crowd capacity are met. To find out whether your venue has a performance license, check with the building manager or owner, such as the local council or school or church offices. You may need to pay extra for this if the venue does not already have a license, or it may be included in the cost of the venue rental. If the venue does not have one and expects you, the renter, to obtain the license on a one-time basis, start the application process as soon as you can; it can be time-consuming.

Business Issues

Tracking revenue and expenditure

It is important that you track revenue produced and expenditure incurred from producing the show. These records help you keep to your anticipated budget and make adjustments if required.

If you are running a not-for-profit group, for example a school, scout, church, or community center group, you need this information to comply with their own organizational requirements. If you are running a private group, you need this information for tax purposes and to track the viability of your business.

You can set up records manually, in a ledger book, or with software such as a spreadsheet or even an accounting package if you are running several groups for profit. See figures 1a–c for examples of what you might need to track.

Keep all receipts; you can always throw them away later, but they are very difficult to replace. Try to avoid combining personal expenditure with that for the group on a single receipt. Annotate the receipt if its purpose is not clear, for example "set materials," "costumes," and so on. It is extremely helpful to store receipts by month, as opposed to slinging them into a shoebox and hoping for the best later. For each year, set up an expanding wallet or a ring binder with labeled pockets.

Income and Expenses – This Year's Show
May 23, 24, 25, 2005

Expenses			
	Quantity	Unit Cost	Total
Showscripts and license			
Scripts	30	2.50	75.00
License	1	30.00	30.00
Performance Venue			
Rental – 5 nights	5	100.00	500.00
Sound technician	5	60.00	300.00
Light technician	5	60.00	300.00
Costumes			
Hats for ladies	4	10.00	40.00
Royal outfit for King (rented)	1	40.00	40.00
Fancy vest/waistcoat	1	15.00	15.00
Pink scarves	20	2.00	40.00
etc.			
Props			
Old phonograph (rented)	1	25.00	25.00
Rubber chickens	4	3.00	12.00
etc.			
Set			
Flower stall (rented)	1	100.00	100.00
Food for set builders	1	20.00	20.00
Backdrop			
Muslin	1	28.00	28.00
Paint	1	29.00	29.00
etc.			
Publicity and Programs			
Programs	600	0.03	18.00
Tickets	600	0.01	6.00
Flyers	100	0.05	5.00
Refreshments			
Drinks	450	0.38	171.00
Candy	400	0.42	168.00
etc.			
Total Expenses			$1,922.00

Figure 1a

24

Income			
	Quantity	Unit Cost	Total
Ticket Sales			
Adult	300	8.00	2,400.00
Child	200	4.00	800.00
Refreshments			
Drinks	425	0.50	212.50
Candy	350	0.60	210.00
Program Sponsors			
Cross Plumbing	1	75.00	75.00
A&J Floral	1	60.00	60.00
etc.			
Total Income			$3,757.50

Figure 1b

Total Profit/Loss	
Total Income	$3,757.50
Total Expenses	$1,922.00
Profit/Loss	$1,835.50

Figure 1c

You will need a lockable cashbox for ticket sales pre- and post-rehearsals and during the shows. You may use it earlier in the sessions if you need to disburse money to group members to buy materials for sets and costumes or for collecting fees. Be sure you can easily keep track of the key, or use a combination lock.

Setting and collecting workshop fees or dues

Workshop fees depend on how much other funding you may have already; if the venue is provided free of charge, your fees obviously do not have to cover its cost. Fees you charge per child per session need to cover costs of running the sessions — venue rent, insurance, materials used, and musical accompaniment. Assume the performance revenue will cover the cost of putting on the show. Seek guidance for how much you should charge by checking into what kids in your area pay for other group leisure activities — swimming lessons, ballet classes, or gymnastics.

25

Remember, you are usually offering two hours per week while other activities may be for only one hour or even thirty minutes. You do not want to be seen as cheap childcare, but neither do you want to put parents off.

In general, it is best to ask parents of new pupils to pay for each individual session until they have decided the child really enjoys the workshops and plans to continue attending. Once the child is firmly part of the group, make it policy to ask for payment upfront for a block of sessions. Explain that missed sessions are not refundable. Six to eight weeks, which is usually a half term or half semester, is a good guideline for determining the length of a block.

If a parent really struggles to pay in advance, allow them to pay weekly, but expect payment for missed sessions.

Calculating ticket prices

You want your ticket sales to cover all costs of production, and ideally produce a bit extra. As you work out your costs, you can start to project your ticket prices, keeping in mind that most of the audience will be drawn from the cast's family, friends, and friends of friends. Also, you cannot sell more tickets per performance than your performance venue can legally hold. So if you are performing three nights in a hall that holds 100, you are limited to a total of 300 tickets, assuming you fill every seat.

First, add up all of your projected costs, and add on 15 percent to cover any unexpected expenditures. Calculate the total number of tickets you think you will be able to sell, and estimate the proportion of full-price tickets and concessionary tickets (child, student, senior citizen) if you are having a tiered pricing system. At this point you will need to start playing with combinations of numbers to determine how much you will need to charge per ticket to cover your projected costs.

If you start the rehearsals months before the show, you can track your actual and projected costs for a while before you decide on your ticket price. Obviously, once you start promoting the show and print the tickets, you must fix the price of your tickets.

Example

You need to raise $1,000 and you believe you can sell sixty child tickets and forty adult tickets. If you price your adult tickets at $15.00 and your child tickets at $7.50, you will raise $1,050, which gives you a bit of a margin should you not sell every single ticket. However, if you price your adult tickets at $14 and your child tickets at $7, you will only raise $980, which is insufficient. If you believe you can sell 200 tickets, your ticket prices can be cut in half.

Recruiting Group Members

If you do not have an established group already in place (for example, a private workshop group, an after-school drama club, a school drama class, a recreational center youth group, scout troop, or church group), or if your group is not large enough to mount a show of twenty to thirty-five performers, you need to recruit new members.

In our experience, the opportunity to be in a "real" show is the greatest recruitment draw for children and young people to join your group. Most of them know what a musical is and the chance to perform in one gives them a concrete goal to work toward as well as an immediate picture of what your group does.

If you have already chosen your musical, simply spread the word — either through your current group members or by advertising — that you need performers. If you don't have an established group and don't wish to commit yourself to a particular script, you can still spread the word that you will be producing a musical.

What to promote about your group

Your announcements, advertisements, and other publicity should focus on your need for performers for an exciting musical. List the name of the musical, or, if still unsure, simply state "an exciting musical." Be sure to provide your contact details, the venue, dates, and times of the first couple sessions, and if possible, information about the planned dates and venue of performance. If your group is new, don't highlight that fact.

Where to promote your group

Where you advertise depends largely on who comprises your group. If you are recruiting for the school drama club or trying to increase the number of students in your drama classes, your avenues of publicity are narrow and obvious. Advertise in the school, via announcements, the school website, and notice boards. Visit the English classes, as drama is closely related to that subject. If you are recruiting at a church, use the church announcements, bulletins, and notice boards.

If however, you are recruiting for a recreational center club, scout group, or your own private group, you may wish to explore a number of different avenues and media including the following:

Websites – If the organization has a website, announce your recruitment drive there. If you are running a private group, consider setting up a website for it.

Posters and flyers – These can be distributed to schools and posted in recreational and leisure centers, libraries, and post offices. See the flyer example in figure 3.

School and radio announcements – Some local stations will carry announcements at no cost to your group, particularly if your group is run free of charge. Check with your local station.

Newspaper advertising and press coverage – If you are running a private, fee-paying group, consider placing an advertisement in the local paper, especially a suburban community paper. You may even be able to get an article in for free. Be sure to provide some photographs if possible. See the sample recruitment press release in figure 2.

Press Release

January 2005

A call has gone out to all young performers, aged 7-11, to join the cast of the musical *Is There a Doctor in the House?* This show will be held in March 2005, and a series of workshops leading up to its production are being held each Saturday from 10 A.M. to 12 P.M. in the Townsville Town Hall.

The show offers a wide variety of singing, dancing, and speaking roles. Everyone who joins the workshops will have a part and the opportunity to learn a number of theatrical skills in the sessions leading up to the show.

For more details, call Adele Lawson at 111-222-3333 or come to a workshop.

Figure 2 – Sample recruitment press release

Young Actors Wanted!

**Adele Lawson's School of Theatre
is currently seeking boys and girls
aged 7–11 for a production
of the musical comedy**

Is There a Doctor in the House?

to be staged at

The Imaginary Theatre, Townsville

in March 2005

Rehearsals are held at

The Local Town Hall

High Street, Townsville 54321

Saturdays 10 A.M. – 12 P.M.

**Everyone who joins will be in the show!
Come to a rehearsal or contact Adele for further details.
Tel: 111-222-3333**

Figure 3 – Sample flyer

Preparing Written Information for Participants and Parents

Information flyer

Once you start to get some interest in your group and begin receiving phone calls or people start showing up at the sessions wanting more information, it is helpful to have on hand a simple one-page flyer describing in more detail your group's theatrical activities and plans. The flyer can be mailed, e-mailed, or handed to potential participants and their parents.

In the flyer, list the place and times for the sessions. Ideally, it will also list performance dates and the venue if the performance will be held in a different place than the rehearsals. If you have not yet decided on a performance venue, simply state that the venue will be confirmed. If possible, include the dates and times of any extra rehearsals that might take place just before the performance. If nothing else, state that some extra rehearsals will take place in the week before the performances begin and that full details will be given as soon as possible. Parents, who may have tight work schedules and several children, each in multiple activities, appreciate as much advance notice as possible.

The flyer should give clear information about fees or group dues and how they are to be paid. For more details, see the section earlier in this chapter, "Setting and collecting workshop fees or dues." The flyer should also clearly indicate if there are costs other than the fees. You don't have to be precise, but state that performers might be expected to provide their own costumes or to pay for those provided, buy their own scripts, or put down a deposit for rented scripts. Parents may become irate if suddenly presented with a bill of $175 for costume rental, even if their child is the star of the show.

This book assumes you will be working with children of a wide range of ages, from six to fifteen. Therefore, you will need help from the parents before and during the performances. Mention this upfront in the flyer. A simple statement such as "As we prepare and perform the show, I will be calling on the parents for a bit of help. Please let me know if you have any particular interest or talent you would like to contribute" will encourage them to volunteer.

If you are working with a group composed of older teens, say sixteen to eighteen with some theatrical experience, you will probably be able to recruit such help from their friends and siblings. However, it doesn't hurt to put the parents in the picture, so they are prepared for any extra time commitments.

Developing good relationships with participants and their parents is important, and the flyer is a good place to start establishing these. In the flyer, make it clear that you are available to speak to at the beginning and end of each session and also by phone. Mention that you look forward to meeting them, and that they are always welcome to stay at the beginning or arrive before the end of a session and observe the group's activities. For an example see the sample information flyer in figure 4.

Registration form
Along with the information flyer, put together a simple registration form. On the form, parents or participants complete details of home address, age, parents' names, contact and emergency phone numbers, and any medical problems. Be sure to leave enough space for information to be filled in clearly, especially e-mail addresses. In this form, outline your expectations for behavior and rehearsal and performance attendance, particularly for sessions running up to the show's opening. You can include a clause that states you reserve the right to ask the child to leave the group if his or her behavior becomes unacceptable or interferes with other children. Provide a place for a parent or guardian to sign, to confirm that he or she accepts the need for standards of behavior. The registration form is a good place to repeat the information regarding payment, particularly to whom checks need to be made out and that missed sessions cannot be refunded. For an example, see the sample registration form in figure 5.

Ongoing communication with performers and parents
In the course of the sessions, regularly send a short letter home. These can inform parents and kids alike about the progress of the rehearsals, due dates for session fees, or the need for off-stage help. If you are asking for fees for blocks of six to eight sessions, the letters should sent just before the beginning of the next block of sessions.

31

Adele Lawson's School of Theatre
23 Any Street, Townsville 54321
Tel: 111-222-3333 – Cell/Mobile: 444-555-6666

Weekly drama workshops for children ages 6–15
All participants will be in a musical show!
Workshops: Saturdays, 10 A.M. – 12 P.M.
The Local Town Hall
High Street, Townsville 54321

Musical production for this year:
Is There a Doctor in the House?
May 20, 21, 22, 2005
(Thursday, Friday, Saturday) 7:30 P.M.
The Imaginary Theatre, Townsville

Adele Lawson's School of Theatre has been running workshops for the past eight years in the Townsville area for children and teenagers ages six to fifteen. We welcome new members and hope you will enjoy the workshops and show.

Workshops run weekly on Saturdays (except school vacations), September – May. Children work with the drama coach and director Adele each week to develop their skills in acting, improvisation, singing, movement, and dance. In May, they put on a full-length show for all their friends and family to see and enjoy.

This year's show, *Is There a Doctor in the House?*, offers a wide range of roles that the performers will enjoy playing.

In the week before the actual performance, three extra rehearsals will be scheduled, each about three to four hours long. Normally they are on the Sunday afternoon and Tuesday and Wednesday evenings before the first night — exact dates to be confirmed as soon as possible.

Cost of each workshop is just $5, payable in advance for an eight-week set of sessions. New members have the option to pay weekly for up to four weeks, which gives the child plenty of time to decide if he or she wishes to continue.

For some roles, each player will be asked to bring ordinary articles of clothing or other items (for example, a button-down shirt, plain trousers, or a bucket and mop). Other costumes will be provided. Each cast member is also asked to pay for the cost of his or her script.

Putting on a musical takes more than just a talented group of performers, it also takes some willing parent volunteers — so if you can help out for one evening during the performances, or would like to use your talents to help with the set, lights, sound, or other backstage role, I would love to hear from you.

Interested? Please fill out the registration sheet and bring to a workshop, or phone Adele for more details.

Figure 4 – Sample information sheet

Adele Lawson's School of Theatre
611 Any Street, Townsville 54321
Tel: 111-222-3333 - Cell/Mobile: 444-555-6666
Member Registration Form (20—Season)

Name: _____

Home telephone:_____ Other telephone: _____

Address:_____

City:_____ State: _____ Postal/zip code: _____

Date of birth:_____ Age:_____ School year: _____

Parent/guardian contact details: Should I need to contact you in an emergency or to inform you of a last minute change of rehearsal, etc., please list details for all parents or guardians who may be contacted.

Parent/guardian (1)
First and last name: _____
Relationship: _____
Address (if different from above): _____

Telephone numbers:
Home:_____Work:_____Mobile/cell:_____

Parent/guardian (2)
First and last name: _____
Relationship: _____
Address (if different from above): _____

Telephone numbers:
Home:_____Work:_____Mobile/cell:_____

Would either parent be willing/available to help out during at one performance or dress rehearsal?   Yes_____   No_____
Best e-mail contact: _____

Other emergency contacts:
Name:_____ Phone: _____
Name:_____ Phone: _____

Medical conditions: Please list any medical conditions, e.g., asthma, allergies, recent illnesses or injuries, etc._____

Acceptance of behavior standards: I understand that members of the Adele Lawson's School of Theatre are expected to behave in a cooperative manner, and if my child shows any unacceptable behavior to other members or adult helpers, he or she will be asked to leave.

Signed:_____ Printed name: _____

Date:_____

Figure 5 – Sample registration form

As the sessions go by, you will normally be sending letters or notices home to the parents reminding them of fees due. These letters are good vehicles to announce your need for particular kinds of help. For example, four months before the show opens, send a letter asking parents to be on the lookout for certain props. If someone secures you some items, include a "thank you" to them in the next letter or notice.

Strategies for Harnessing the Parental Workforce

It is important that the parents know that you will be asking for, and expecting, help. They may assume that you have other sources of help. If they have never been involved with amateur dramatics, they may simply be unaware of the need for help before and during the show.

From most parents, you will require only a minimal commitment of time, which makes the choice for them to become involved that much easier. Luckily, a few parents usually have an interest in amateur theatre themselves and will want to be involved. These are the people you need to call on to be your set builders, callboys, prompts and lighting assistants, as you will need them for several sessions.

From the outset be polite, but clear and specific, about your need for help. Alert the parents and mention when you speak to them before or after sessions that you will be approaching them for help and inviting them to volunteer. Always seem confident that you will get enough help and that those involved will enjoy it.

If you have a flyer for your group, include a couple of sentences that will prepare the parents for your eventual call for help. See the section above, "Providing information to parents." In your regular letters, ask specifically for any immediate help (does anyone know where we can find an iron bedstead?) and warm the parents up for long-term requests.

When someone does mention they may be interested in helping out, even in a vague way, it is most important that you listen to, remember, and follow up on that offer. People may feel slighted if they think an offer of help has been rebuffed. They then vow silently never to volunteer again. Keep a clipboard and pen handy before and after the sessions, and write down the names and numbers of any volunteers.

If someone offers to do a big job, such as callboy or prompt, it's worthwhile to phone them separately and discuss the realities of the role as soon as possible. Reconfirm any offers of help closer to the time it is needed. Even the most well-intentioned volunteers can get caught up in changing circumstances. Someone who had every intention to run the lights six months ago may be working night shifts by the time the performances begin. Keep some backups in mind.

The sample 36-week rehearsal schedule included in chapter 3 outlines when requests are best made for particular tasks. Also, see chapter 14, "Putting It All Together," which outlines clearly what roles will need to be filled by adults, explains how involved they will be, and discusses how to set up help sign-up sheets (rotas) to get commitments from your (hopefully) many volunteers.

Things You Will Need to Prepare and Bring to the Sessions

Some of the following things you will need for almost every session; others you will bring at particular points in the rehearsal schedule.

Attendance list, spare information flyers and registration forms, cashbox with float

These items are particularly useful if you are running private sessions or a club. An attendance list will help you record who has come to your sessions and their payment status, if relevant. Take attendance at each session so you can track your loyal members. It certainly never hurts to recognize consistent attendance with an announcement and simple prize.

Information forms and registration forms are useful for new members, or for people to take home to other interested parties.

A cashbox, with a float for making change, is useful if you charge new members for individual sessions, payable on the day, before they decide to join the group and pay for a block of sessions. It will also be useful when you are selling tickets closer to the performance date.

Master and other backstage scripts

You will need to claim one script for your sole use as the "Master" script. In this script, record any line changes and cuts. As

35

you progress through the rehearsals, add blocking, notes on character, and sound and lighting cues. Label this script clearly and don't let anyone else even breathe on it!

If your script is small, for example, half-letter size in the U.S.A. or A5 in the U.K., there will not be enough room in the margins for all your notes. It is time-consuming, but worthwhile, to make a master script where each page is set within the page of a strong spiral notebook, which gives you plenty of room for notes. To make a director's script, from the bottom outside corner of each notebook page, cut out a rectangle the same height and width as the script. Then use clear tape to affix each script page into the cutout section of the notebook page. This way you will be able to read both sides of the script page and have plenty of space to record notes and changes on the remaining notebook paper. See figure 6.

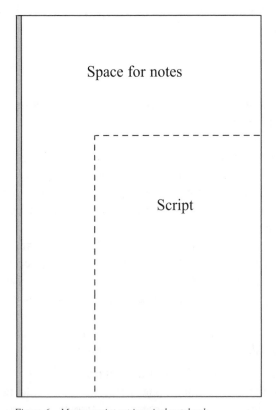

Figure 6 – Master script set in spiral notebook

In addition to the master script, you will need suitably marked scripts for the prompt, callboy, and lighting and sound assistants.

Actors' scripts

Once you have selected the musical and are ready to audition the parts, try to provide one copy for each cast member. If possible, try to provide a full script for everyone in the show. It will help them understand the entire show and their part in it. You may not want to hand scripts out for them to keep until they are expected to start learning their lines, about half-way through the rehearsal schedule. Until then, make sure you collect them all at the end of each session.

If you have purchased copies of the scripts for the group, ask the performers to pay for the individual copies you give them, assuming your situation allows this. Parents are usually willing to pay for scripts. Many children have a somewhat cavalier attitude toward "free" materials, and this payment encourages them to take more responsibility for their scripts. If they lose the script or destroy it to the point it's unusable, charge for a replacement if possible. Scripts don't fall apart by themselves, end up drenched in Coke by themselves, or get ripped and stepped on by themselves — the performers do it!

If performing rights oblige you to rent, not purchase, scripts, they usually must be returned to the publisher after the show is completed. Upon receipt, number all scripts. Make a master list of these numbers, and beside each number record the name of the cast member who has been given that script. Insist that the performer's parent signs for the script, and ask for a returnable deposit, which will cover the replacement cost if the child fails to return the script in good condition.

Song sheets

Song or lyric sheets are simply typed sheets with the lyrics to all songs, one set per cast member. If your performing rights permit this, it is helpful to provide these sheets, which contain all the lyrics of the songs in the show, separate from the dialog script. It is helpful to annotate the stanzas with numbers, so you can easily give clear instructions — for example, "start with the second stanza." If you cannot create separate song sheets, just use the scripts and instruct as required, "Now try 'Who Will Buy,' page 63."

Spare scripts and spare song sheets

You will need spare scripts in the case some actors are absent and members of the chorus, who may not have scripts but only lyric sheets, need to read in the part.

You will also need spare scripts for performers who forget to bring their own to rehearsal. Some kids have no problem remembering to bring their scripts or song sheets, but others have immense difficulty organizing themselves and their possessions. There is no point in getting annoyed about this. To preserve your own sanity, keep some spare scripts and song sheets available for those who have forgotten them.

If you do need to provide a spare script or song sheet to your forgetful actor, it is helpful to write their name down on a spare whiteboard or other display — explain it helps you both to remember to get it back and saves you the anguish of seeing your spare sets disappear as well.

A "boom box" stereo cassette/CD player with adequate speakers

If you are not using a plug adapter, bring plenty of spare batteries. If you are using a plug adapter, bring an extension cord.

Song recording and/or accompaniment track of show (cassette tape and/or CD)

You can use these to teach the songs and as substitution for live music throughout the rehearsals. If you are using only an accompaniment track during the show, you will eventually use the "instrumental only" side while your cast belts out the songs. CDs are convenient for finding one particular song. Both can be rewound or reset to a particular point in a song, which is handy when you are working on a particularly challenging part of a song.

Before you leave the house, check that the tape or CD is actually in the case.

Cast list and matrix of roles

Once you cast the show, make up a cast list for reference and bring it to each rehearsal. It will help you keep track of who is playing what, particularly if you have some actors playing multiple chorus roles or other small parts. The cast list (along with the role matrix discussed below) also helps assign roles if someone is absent and someone else needs to read the part. This can be an excellent opportunity for someone who is in the chorus to gain experience with a larger role.

It is also helpful, especially if you have some absent actors, to have a matrix or other list that will show you at a glance which character is in which scene. Most musicals are in two long acts, and many don't have the formal scene breaks you would find in stage plays. In this case, it is helpful to go through the script and mark natural scenes and record exactly which characters are in them. See figure 7 for an example of a matrix.

Act, scene		I, i	I, ii	I, iii	I, iv	I, v	I, vi	etc.
Location		Hot	St	Bch	Hosp	Bch	Hot	
Character	Cast Member							
Sad Sam	Jenny P.	X	X			X	X	
Jolly John	Peter J.		X	X	X		X	
Mrs. Hotchkiss	Andrea	X			X	X	X	
etc.								

Figure 7 – Character and scene matrix

Stage props, costumes, scenery, lights, musical instruments, etc.

As the sessions continue and the performance date nears, you will also need to provide either rehearsal or real props, costumes, and scenery.

Tickets and promotional flyers

You will be selling tickets before and after the rehearsals leading up to the performance. For these rehearsals, you need to bring tickets, a ticket sales record sheet if you are having a contest, and promotional flyers. If you are not already bringing a cashbox with a float for collecting fees, you will need to bring one to hold the ticket money.

Chapter 3

Planning Your Rehearsal Schedule

Before you start the workshops, draw up an audition and rehearsal schedule. Even if you are inexperienced and the entire project seems abstract, it is worthwhile to plan a schedule.

For rehearsal purposes, review the script. You are trying to predict — which is difficult — how long it will take to rehearse the entire show. You need to allow enough time to rehearse all parts of the show equally. It's easy to get bogged down in act 1, rehearsing it to perfection, while you run out of time for act 2, which may be shorter but more complicated in terms of dance numbers, physical action, or character development.

Therefore, review the script and see how you can break it up into sections or "chunks" that each require about the same amount of rehearsal. These sections do not necessarily equal the "scenes" of the actual script.

For planning purposes, keep in mind that act 1 is generally longer than act 2. Solo and duets usually require only minimal dance movement and obviously only a few performers, so these numbers usually take less time to rehearse and polish. Dialog scenes with only a few principals also do not take as long to rehearse as scenes with several characters. In contrast, big dance numbers take lots of time to learn and rehearse.

For example, in your play, you may find that act 1 has no scene demarcations at all, but breaks down into six sections, and that act 2 breaks down into four, giving you a total of ten sections.

You can give each section a number as we do in the sample rehearsal schedule at the end of this chapter, or use page numbers, for example, act 1, scene 3, pp. 20–24. If you do assign numbers to the sections as we have done, record the corresponding act, scene and/or page numbers at the front of your script.

Types of Rehearsals

In our sample schedule, most sessions consist of different types of rehearsals. However, you and your group will refer to the entire session as a rehearsal. We recommend that you mix up the types of rehearsal within a given session, as this variety makes it more interesting for young performers. If your sessions are only one hour in length, you can realistically only conduct one or possibly two types of rehearsals each session. If you have a separate musical director or choreographer, you may need to schedule certain sessions that concentrate only on music or dance. Here are some of the different types of rehearsals:

Read-through rehearsal – Often the first formal rehearsal, the cast sits in a circle and reads through the script in its entirety. We would counsel you against this. Because most of the cast has seen the video or received a vivid explanation of the action from you, they know the general story, and they will find sitting around reading through the script boring, and having to listen to other people reading through the script even more boring. And once they are bored, you've got trouble, with the unhappy result that you will spend more time "shushing" your performers than working with them.

Walk-through rehearsal – Instead, at your first formal rehearsal, we recommend you have the actors walk-through the action, reading the parts, singing the numbers but without instruction from you regarding blocking.

Singing rehearsals – These focus on preparation of songs. Usually the musical director will run these. However, we recommend you include a singing rehearsal at every two-hour rehearsal session even if the musical director isn't present. If you have a recording of the music, you can run these yourself.

Dance rehearsals – These are used to prepare dance numbers. If you have recorded music for the actors to move to and you know the basic steps yourself, you don't necessarily need the choreographer to attend each of these. We recommend you include a dance rehearsal in every two-hour rehearsal session.

41

Dialog (or acting) rehearsals – These cover dialog scenes. Each two-hour rehearsal session should have some dialog rehearsal.

Principals' rehearsals – Use these rehearsals to prepare those scenes with only a few actors. They should be held outside normal workshop hours, and are particularly useful for romantic scenes and solo or duet song numbers.

Speed rehearsal – At this rehearsal the entire show is performed with the actors speaking and moving as quickly as possible. This should be done after all lines have been learned. The performers usually love it. This approach can help recapture performance energy, which tends to drag toward the end of the rehearsal period.

Technical rehearsal – During this the show is performed so that all lighting, sound, and other special effects can be rehearsed, along with prop, furniture, and scenery changes. If there are many costume changes or fast costume changes, a technical rehearsal can include using costumes. Sometimes parts of scenes are skipped if there are no technical cues or fast costume changes going on backstage.

Dress rehearsal – During this final rehearsal the show is performed with all technical effects, props, costumes, and makeup.

Accommodating the Schedules of Your Choreographer and Musical Director

If you have a separate musical director and/or choreographer, they will probably not attend every rehearsal. Try to meet with them as soon as possible to schedule music rehearsals or dance rehearsals they can attend in addition to the dress rehearsals and performances. You can usually survive with the musical director attending one out of every six sessions, although ideally he or she would attend one out of every three rehearsals. Your choreographer will need about the same schedule. If you devote a rehearsal to singing or dancing alone, swap any acting/singing/dancing that you would have done during that time to the previous or following week.

During music rehearsals, you may get restless cries from some of your lead performers of "Can't we do some acting now?" An ideal solution is to have a second rehearsal room where you can work on dialog scenes. If you don't have the ideal situation, don't let it interfere with your music rehearsal. If leads are not performing a leading role in a group scene, insist that they learn the song and dance anyway and become part of the chorus for that rehearsal if not for the actual performance. If nothing else, they may stand in for an absent chorus member, or they may go to the back of the room and learn their lines. Chorus members usually don't mind relaxing for a while and watching the solo scenes.

Structuring Rehearsals for Maximum Involvement of Everyone Attending

One of our workshop goals is to keep all participants involved and on-stage as much as possible. However, almost no script has all thirty-five cast members on stage non-stop. So you will have actors off-stage on a regular basis. This can be especially challenging when you have a captive audience, for example a drama class in secondary school or private group that pays for each session.

In any case, it is important that you make sure there is something for everyone to do during the rehearsal and that everyone feels as involved as possible. Although you need to concentrate on directing the actors who are actually on-stage at a given moment, you also must give the chorus and those playing minor roles something to do while waiting their turn on-stage.

To help solve this challenge, we recommend that you try, as much as possible, to include a variety of activities in *every* session, in which *most* of your group can participate. Because our rehearsals devote lots of time to singing the songs and learning and practicing the dance routines, watching a dialog scene in rehearsal can come as a positive relief to the tired chorus members. However, if you announce that they will be asked for comments on the acting of their peers and be expected to go on-stage on cue for the next number, they still have to pay attention.

As much as possible, direct those performers not in the scene to come out into the audience area with you; don't allow them to wander around backstage unsupervised. Throughout our discussion of directing dialog scenes in chapter 9, we describe different ways of keeping off-stage performers engaged with the workshop activities and focused on the action of the musical.

43

Other Common Situations Affecting Rehearsal Management and Scheduling

Scenes with few actors

It is inevitable that scenes with only two to three actors, particularly romantic scenes, will need some work, preferably in the presence of on-lookers. If you are running a workshop, your participants (and their parents) will take exception to your scheduling entire workshop sessions for only a few actors. It is usually best to ask the leads to stay for an extra hour after one or two of the regular sessions for small group scenes.

If you are rehearsing the play during a normal classroom period, you have no option but to have the entire group in the room at the same time. Rehearse with the principals while the others have a quiet break. Try to explore the option of scheduling rehearsals with the principals during a lunch break or before/after regular school hours.

Absent actors

This can be a common dilemma, and can be particularly irritating if you have had no notice. Don't change your plans for the day. Your cast list and scene matrix comes in handy here. Simply ask another actor, usually one with a chorus role, to "read in" the part for the day. Tell him or her you expect them to put as much effort as possible into the reading, as it is a chance to practice a larger part. The actor, usually, will be thrilled to be in the limelight.

If someone's dance partner is absent, instruct the dancer to imagine that partner, perhaps advising, "Now sashay around Mr. Nobody." Your dancers will usually find this as much fun — and often easier — as working with real people. If a member of a group of singers or dancers is absent, ask the others to imagine that the person is actually there, or ask a spare principal to stand in.

If a chorus number is led by a character who is missing that day, it may be easier if you take the role while the rest of the chorus sings around you.

Performers who join the group partway through rehearsals

If your private group is successful, you will have people wanting to join throughout the rehearsal period. If you are running a school club or class, you will always have new students moving in. By being flexible with the chorus parts, you can usually accommodate new arrivals up until the last few weeks before the show.

New members can quite easily join chorus numbers with simple dances. If you have all the dancers/singers working in pairs, change one of them into a threesome. An existing group member will usually be thrilled to be asked to teach the new member the dances, so normally you do not need to provide one-to-one coaching on top of all your other activities. The new member, of course, must accept that the major roles have been cast, but explain that being in the chorus is a vital experience for anyone interested in musical theatre.

For more information on helping new members become part of the group, see the section, "Integrating New Members into the Group" in chapter 4.

Members dropping out

If you are running any kind of recreational group, no law says group members have to stay for the duration. Kids have short attention spans and often plenty of activities to choose from, so you may lose a few during the season. This is usually not a problem early in the rehearsal schedule, as you can move people around into different roles. Later on, you can accommodate sudden gaps in leading roles by "promoting" chorus actors who show the potential to do the part. For dances, you may need to convert some pairs into trios.

For leading roles, always have some backups in mind, in case something happens in the final days of rehearsals and a leading character can't do the performances. The possibility, however remote, of having to bring in a new lead at the last minute is another reason why it is worthwhile to insist all the actors know all of the show.

It may be useful to make a note of any school or amateur groups who have done the show recently. In an emergency, you may be able to pick up a leading lady or man who would like to be a star one more time.

However, for emergency cover, you can always use someone who has read in the part at your rehearsals. In the worst-case scenario of sudden severe illness on the day of performance, you will have to send someone on-stage reading from a script: for the sake of all those who have diligently rehearsed, the show must go on. And the youngster taking on the emergency role will love the spotlight and always get heartfelt applause.

Understudies

We find it is not a good idea to have formal understudies. The actual lead will quite naturally want to do all the performances and the understudies will be disappointed if they don't get a chance to perform the role. By having all the actors know the show, and using spare actors to read in for any absent actors, you will usually have someone who can step into the role at the last minute, even if he or she needs to use a script.

Extra time in a session

Sometimes the scenes you rehearse do not take up the entire session. An extra five or ten minutes can provide your group an opportunity to try a game. See chapter 5, or appendix 3 for game ideas.

Also, it never hurts to run a dance routine one more time.

Sample 36-Week Rehearsal Schedule

We have put together a sample rehearsal schedule based on thirty-six two-hour sessions, including a few extra rehearsals right before the performance. We have indicated which rehearsals might be "singing only" rehearsals in the cases where the musical director can come to only every third or sixth rehearsal.

For the sake of our example, we have decided the play breaks down into sixteen sections, eight in each act. We have also assigned letters of the alphabet to the songs. A – H have been given to the chorus numbers and I – P to the solo/duet numbers. You may wish to do the same, or use the names of the songs or their numbers as listed in the score, in your plan. Record the names of the songs with their assigned letters or numbers in the front of your script.

Our sample plan has a total of sixteen sections and sixteen musical numbers. Your plan may have any number of sections and any number of song and dance routines. The goal is to distribute the rehearsal time so all parts of the musical receive enough attention and you end up with a wonderful performance. See figure 8, "Sample 36-Week Rehearsal Schedule."

Sample 36-Week Rehearsal Schedule

Session	Information to be sent home to parents	Activities during the sessions	Activities outside the sessions
1	Collect registration forms for new participants.Ask for updates from returning participants. Fees due reminder for following week.Schedule of next break. Announce show dates if possible.	Talk briefly about the play, plot and characters. Hand out song sheets or scripts. Run through songs A, B, C, and D as a warm-up. Learn lyrics of big song A. Break (10 minutes). Teach stage areas and actor positions. Learn and run dance routine to song A. Run routine. Collect sheets or scripts.	If you are building your own, start set design. Determine set layout for blocking purposes. Search for and book performance venue if you haven't already done so. Discuss scheduling and availability with musical director for audition workshops and rehearsals and plan accordingly.
2		Hand out scripts or song sheets. Introduce the musical, either by viewing the video or through other activities. If time permits, work on songs and run routine A.	
Auditions (4 sessions) Musical director should attend at least one session.			
3		Run through songs E, F, G, and H as a warm-up. Learn song B. Run routine to A (dance audition). Discuss improvisation of a scene from the show. Break. Groups work on improvised scene and perform improvisations, repeating the scene several times to give everyone a chance to be in any role they want to audition for. Sing A and B. Allow volunteers to sing one solo verse each (singing audition).	If renting scenery, arrange as soon as the venue is confirmed.
4	Start talking to parents/send letter to recruit help with set-building (if needed), prompt, callboy, costume making. Find out if anyone has a van if you will need help with transportation.	Run through songs I, J, K, and L as a warm-up. Learn song C. Learn dance B. Break. Give out scripts to the performers to use for an audition scene. Divide into groups according to the number of characters in that scene. As groups work on their scenes, observe them. Run dance A and B (dance audition). Send scripts home to practice audition scene.	

Figure 8

Session	Information to be sent home to parents	Activities during the sessions	Activities outside the sessions
5		Run dance B. Ask the performers to get into groups, quickly practice the assigned audition scenes from the previous week, and then perform them. Play the game, "Who would you cast?" and collect the sheets before the break. Break. Discuss results from "Who would you cast?" Run through songs M, N, O, and P. Ask those who wish to audition for a major singing role to sing a solo verse from one of the principals' songs. Repeat songs as necessary until everyone who wishes to has sung a solo verse from one of the songs. Learn song D if there is time. Ask actors to take a set of lyrics home and practice one of the songs for a singing audition next session.	
6	End of first set of sessions; next week will be a break. Reminder of break and fees due for next session by (reasonable date).	Arrange for musical director to attend this session to help you select singers if otherwise unavailable for auditions. Form groups and ask each to make up a routine to song C. Meanwhile take individuals out to do singing audition of song chosen last session. Perform group routines (dance audition). Outline a scenario for a second improvised scene, involving the same or different characters from those in week 3. Break. Actors work on improvised scenes then perform scenes (acting audition). Sing through principals' songs. Ask any individual for whom you have a major part in mind to sing verses of an appropriate song. Then allow everyone who wishes to sing a solo verse to do so (singing audition).	Prepare floor plan for blocking rehearsals. Draw up props list and begin planning how you will obtain them.

Cast the show; blocking rehearsals (6 sessions)

All sessions begin with a singing warm-up of a song from the show and end with a concluding number. Musical director should attend two sessions, which should concentrate on musical numbers with the assigned dance routines.

Figure 8 continued

48

Session	Information to be sent home to parents	Activities during the sessions	Activities outside the sessions
7	Reminder of fees that are due. Start asking for props to be set aside.	Announce cast. Walk through the whole show without stopping. Allow cast to move freely. For musical numbers, all those involved should go on-stage and sing (and dance if you have taught the routine). Have break at the usual time. Ask those not on-stage to sing from off-stage or from the audience.	
8		Review theatrical basics with a game or two. Introduce idea of stage business. Learn dance C. Sing and dance A, B, C; learn song E. Break. Block for act 1, sections 1–4. Include any dances covered or stand and sing the number.	If renting set, find supplier: Get full details and measure that the equipment will fit into the venue properly.
9		** Learn dance D. Run through dances A, B, and C. Learn song F. Break. Block act 1, sections 5–8. Include any dances covered or ask performers to stand and sing the number.	
10		Learn dance E. Run through A, B, C, and D. Break. Block act 2, sections 1–4. Include any dances covered or ask performers to stand and sing the number.	
11		Learn dance F. Run through B, C, D, and E. Break. Block act 2, sections 5–8. Include any dances covered or ask the performers to stand and sing the number.	
12	End of second set of sessions. Reminder note of any break, and when fees are next due.	* Run the whole show to rehearse blocking. Put in any dances covered and stand and sing the other numbers.	

"Work" the action (12 sessions)

Complete dance routines and work through dialog scenes, taking each scene slowly and stopping whenever you want to improve on something.

Session	Information to be sent home to parents	Activities during the sessions	Activities outside the sessions
13	Reminder of fees due; dates of show and technical/dress rehearsals that will be at times/days of week different from the usual session.	Tell cast to start learning lines — each week, learn what has been rehearsed that session. Run dance C, D, E, and F. Learn dance G and H. Break. Work act 1, sections 1–2, Run any dances in these scenes. Run A and B if not in the scenes.	

Figure 8 continued

49

Session	Information to be sent home to parents	Activities during the sessions	Activities outside the sessions
14		Run G and I. Learn dance H. Break. Work act 1, sections 3–4. Run or put in C and D.	
15		** Run G, H, and I. Learn dance J. Break. Work act 1, sections 5–6. Run/put in any numbers already learned.	
16		Run G and H. Learn dance K. Break. Work act 1, sections 7–8. Run/put in any numbers already learned.	
17		Run E. Learn dance L. Practice any big numbers in act 1.	
18	End of third set of sessions. Reminder of any break between the sessions and when fees are next due.	* Run act 1 with musical numbers in place.	
19	Reminder of fees due. Ask the parents to help their children learn their lines or lyrics.	Run A and B. Learn M. Work act 2, sections 1–2.	Draw up list of scenes in the show (running order) and enlarge as much as possible, either by photocopying or putting on poster paper. Display at rehearsals and performances.
20		Run C and D. Learn N. Work act 2, sections 3–4.	
21		** Run E and F. Learn O. Work act 2, sections 5–6.	
22		Run G and H. Learn P. Work act 2, sections 7–8.	
23		Practice any big numbers in act 2.	
24	End of fourth set of sessions. Reminder of break dates and when fees are due.	* Run act 2 with musical numbers.	Mark up separate scripts for prompter and musical director/musicians. Take photos of selected scenes with costumes for publicity.

Polish the show (6 sessions)

Run through entire sections, moving straight into dance numbers. Don't stop the action, but give brief notes afterwards. From now on: Actors are not allowed scripts on-stage. Stage props should be used. Actors start to be responsible for scene changes, with show crew eventually chosen. A prompt should be used. He/she can be recruited from the cast as required. Musical director should attend as often as possible.

Session	Information to be sent home to parents	Activities during the sessions	Activities outside the sessions
25	Reminder of fees.	Polish act 1, sections 1–4. Begin recruiting the core stage crew from the cast. Ask them to watch the action and start planning scene changes during the next four rehearsals.	Prepare callboy script.

Figure 8 continued

Session	Information to be sent home to parents	Activities during the sessions	Activities outside the sessions
26	List of costumes/props/ makeup and how they will be provided.	Polish act 1, sections 5–8.	Arrange for any publicity; print tickets. Design and arrange for printing of programs, but wait until the last possible minute to print in case of any unexpected changes. Invite cast to proof the spelling of their names. They become very upset if their names are incorrect.
27		Ask musical director and pianist, if using live music, to attend. Polish act 1.	Start sessions to build scenery if doing your own. Continue until completed.
28		Polish act 2, sections 1–4.	
29		Polish act 2, sections 5–8. Finalize core stage crew and stage crew leader(s).	
30	End of fifth set of sessions. Reminder of fees due. Ask for help selling tickets/ announce contest.	Ask musical director/pianist, if using live music, to attend. Polish act 2.	Meet with musical director/pianist to discuss and mark up score.

Pull show together

Start to prepare for scene changes and to incorporate other technical effects into the show.
Reinforce the "no scripts on-stage" rule. Start to sell tickets at rehearsals.
Start using stage crew and callboy at rehearsals.

Session	Information to be sent home to parents	Activities during the sessions	Activities outside the sessions
31	Reminder of fees due, that tickets are now on sale/ prices, importance of helping fill the audience. Ask for show sign-up sheets to be filled. Announce dates, times, venues of final rehearsals. Provide map to venue if different from workshop. Send flyer for show.	No musicians need to attend. Rehearse all scene changes in act 1, concentrating on the beginnings and endings of each scene. Repeat. Record who does what during scene changes. Use any cast member as prompt.	Appoint official prompt and callboy for dress rehearsal and performances. Finalize program and send to printer.
32		Rehearse all scene changes in act 2, as in session 31. Use any cast members as prompt.	
33		Run through entire show, with scene changes. Use any cast members as prompt.	Mark up scripts for lighting and sound technicians. Arrange for van for the following session if any scenery moving is to be done.
34		Run through whole show, in costume, using props. Use any cast members as prompt.	Collect any rented sets, costumes, props and take to performance venue.

Figure 8 continued

Session	Information to be sent home to parents	Activities during the sessions	Activities outside the sessions
35		Technical rehearsal — finalize lighting and sound, scene changes, costumes, props, and quick costume changes, stopping and starting as required. Use official, non-cast member as prompt Musical director/pianist should attend.	Practice with microphones if using. Collect programs.
36		Full dress rehearsal — perform with costumes, props, scenery, all musicians, prompt, callboy, and technicians.	Pay bills. Determine winner of ticket competition.

Performances!

Post-performance workshop — share information about next season's show; play improvisations and games.

* If musical director is available only every six rehearsals, make this rehearsal singing only; adjust other rehearsals to accommodate dialog practice.

** If your musical director is available every three weeks, make this rehearsal singing and dancing only; adjust other rehearsals to accommodate dialog practice.

Figure 8 continued

52

Chapter 4
Running the Sessions

Recording Attendance and Other Information

From the first session, maintain an attendance list or register for each session. On this list, record payment information beside each attendance mark, so you can have that quick chat with a parent or post a reminder if payments are not up-to-date. If you are comfortable using software such as Microsoft Excel, it is easy to format and print off sheets. Alternatively, use a record book with a column drawn in for each session.

Collect registration forms from each participant so you have some basic information about each child, including name, address, phone number, emergency phone number(s), and whether they have any medical problems (such as asthma) that might require attention during the session. Ask returning members to fill out new forms so you have any new phone numbers or addresses.

Although you may have provided each participant with a flyer giving information about the performance dates, keep reminding the group of those dates throughout the sessions. Ask them, "Are these dates on your family calendar?" or "Are they on the refrigerator door?" Constant reminders help avoid the problem of the leading lady informing you, two weeks before the show, that her family will be leaving for vacation on your opening night.

Getting to Know Your Group (First Session)

Even if your group has been established for several years, the first session should focus on helping any new members feel comfortable, setting the ground rules of your group, discussing the new project of the next show, and starting to work on the musical numbers.

If you haven't yet decided on a show, discuss the possibilities, talk about some of the characters group members might play or costumes they might wear.

Presenting an overview of the show

Most new members will have come because of your flyers, or because they know someone in the group. Explain that your plan is to have everyone be part of the show, and that chorus numbers are particularly important to a show's success. Briefly describe the show's characters, setting, and plot, mentioning any famous songs that may be familiar to the group. Announce the performance dates. Explain how the auditions work.

If you haven't decided on a show, you can still spend time explaining the different activities that will take place over the rehearsal period. Simply spend more time working on the musical number from another or potential show, or more time on playing theatre games.

Making the group comfortable

If the group is new, or has any new members at all, do some icebreakers. (Two are explained below.) New members need help in learning the names of the "old" members. By asking everyone to participate equally, you help avoid cliques.

Icebreaker 1

This activity is very easy and helps introduce everyone quickly.
1. Everyone sits in a circle, including you.
2. Everyone quickly learns the name of the players to their right and left.
3. Go around the circle clockwise. Each player in turn says his or her name and introduces the person to his or her left. For example: "My name's Emily, and this is my friend Tom."
4. Tom then says, "My name's Tom, and this is my friend Lizzie," again introducing the person on his left. Lizzie then says, "My name's Lizzie, and this is my friend Lee."
5. Continue until everyone is introduced.

Icebreaker 2

This activity is more challenging — a good way to see who can learn lines quickly!

1. Sit in a circle.
2. Start in a clockwise direction, although you may want to change direction midway through the game.
3. The first person says, "My name is Emily and I like drama."
4. The second person indicates the first person and says, "This is Emily and she likes drama. My name's Tom and I like basketball."
5. The third person indicates the first two people and says, This is Emily; she likes drama. This is Tom and he likes basketball. My name's Lizzie and I like chocolate."
6. Continue until everyone is mentioned. The last person may have to remember thirty names and preferences!

If the group is large, these games can become a bit tedious. About half-way through, go back to where you started, this time moving counterclockwise, so no one has to remember — or listen to — the full list of participants.

Singing a warm-up and song

Direct the group in singing the first four songs of the show. This is something they will be doing at every single session, so it's a good idea to start with the first meeting of the season. Sing loudly yourself!

Teach the first song of the show. See the section, "Singing," in chapter 10.

Theatrical basics

Introduce or review the stage area and actor positions, and play some of the games. See chapter 5 for details.

Teaching and running a musical number

Teach the dance steps of the first musical number of the show. If you haven't selected a show, run a number from another show you have done, or from one that you are thinking about doing.

Now is the time to start observing: Who can learn quickly? Who moves well? Sings loudly and in tune?

Setting the ground rules with the group

Your group members need to understand that you rightly expect a certain standard of behavior and courtesy toward one another and toward yourself. This includes being on time and ready to participate, listening, not throwing prima donna tantrums, and clearing up at the end of the session.

Do expect, as with any group of young people, a certain amount of chaos, disorganization, and less-than-immediate response when you give instructions. Try to make instructions as precise, specific, and concrete as possible. The direction, "Come downstage and put your scripts in a pile right *here*" works much better than the announcement, "I need your scripts." The instruction, "You four — Sam, Joe, Carolyn, and Sophie — go over to stage right. You other four go to stage left," works better than, "Divide into two groups on different sides of the stage."

Normally, if your actors are busy chatting and you want them all to go up on stage, expect to repeat that instruction several times. You can, of course, work on conditioning the group to your own style: for example, you will say things twice only and then — too late! See chapter 15 for more tips on working with young performers.

A Typical Session

Before and after the session

If you are running a workshop and your schedule permits, be available for about ten minutes at the beginning and end of each session. This gives parents an opportunity to talk to you about any concerns, and for you to speak to them about any issues you may be concerned about and to talk to any new members. Try to meet each parent and make sure they know who *you* are. When possible, introduce them to other members of your directorial team, such as the musical director or choreographer, or other parents who may already be helping out in some capacity. Encourage the parents to stay or come back early so they can observe part of a session. Their kids may not like this, but most parents appreciate the invitation.

Ask them how they think things are going. You may receive copious unsolicited advice on many subjects. However, it is at these informal encounters you often get offers of help.

Starting and ending times

It is helpful if you set an example by starting and ending workshop sessions on time. Parents and kids alike often have tight schedules and are not impressed to arrive at a venue and to find the group leader missing. Afterward they both may need to go on to another activity or simply home to a family meal, and they can become resentful and anxious if the session goes on longer than expected.

Your group needs to follow your example: be on time, stay for the full session, and be picked up on time. If they need to arrive late, leave early, miss a session, encourage them to give you some advance warning. If a participant is frequently not picked up on time, which automatically presents you with a security issue, consider asking the parent to take the child out of the group. You may need to think about changing the information in the flyer to cover this situation if it becomes persistent with a particular set of parents.

The break

If you are running a two-hour session, by the end of the first hour, the group will need and want a break. If your rehearsal venue allows food, encourage them to bring snacks — it will help renew their energy level and enable them to relax and talk informally with each other. Announce the break as lasting ten minutes, but expect it to take them fifteen minutes to eat their snacks, chat, and go to the restroom before they actually reconvene.

Over time, it is helpful to find out — usually just by asking at the break — if group members attend or have attended dance classes, singing, or music lessons. Perhaps they sing in a church choir or take part with their parents in an amateur group. Even if they do not get large roles, this information will help you plan the singing and dancing numbers.

Clearing up at the end of the session

Some clearing up usually needs to take place at the end of each session; chairs may need to be straightened and stacked, the boom box unplugged, props stowed, scripts collected.

Don't assume that the kids will, of their own volition, help you to put things away at the end of the session. It's not in their nature, so schedule it into each session. You must also take the time to direct them to do it properly and supervise the task. The alternative is to be left with the kids disappearing happily down the corridor, leaving you with a mess.

Another thing you need to anticipate, which can be a particular problem if you use a rented rehearsal space for only a few hours a week, is that kids tend to forget to take home their personal belongings. If they arrive with a coat, they may easily forget to take it home with them, particularly if they become hot during the rehearsal or change into a costume. So remind them to remember what personal belongings they have brought and to collect them.

If you are in a rented venue, check that it has trash cans or bins in your rehearsal area. If not, bring along some bin liners to collect trash.

Preparing for clearing up

At the beginning of the session, ask the group to look around the room and to remember how it appears. Emphasize that they will be leaving it in the same — if not better — condition. Stress to the group that clearing things away and leaving the room in order is part of the session, that the final five minutes will be devoted to this task, that everyone will have a role, and that no one will leave until the room is declared in satisfactory order by you. Also, stress that they need to take home all the things they brought with them.

Finally, have a plan in mind for how to indicate that the session is over and the participants can leave. Of course, in a school situation, the group can return to their seats and wait until the bell rings. For private sessions, perhaps where chairs must be stacked before you leave, you may need to state that no one leaves the rehearsal area until the room is tidy, the chairs are stacked, and they all have their belongings in hand.

Supervising clearing up

When the time arrives for tidying up the rehearsal area, *avoid* phrases like "Everyone help stack chairs against the wall" or "Will someone please unplug the stereo and pack it away?" In the minds of your group, the following equations spontaneously and immutably occur:

"Everyone" does not equal me. "Everyone" equals everyone else.

"Someone" does not equal me. "Someone" equals someone else.

Therefore, you must be prepared to direct individual participants to do particular tasks. Have a clear idea in your own mind of what needs to be done and how many people are needed for each task. This becomes easier after a couple of sessions.

You can then look at the group and ask specific individuals to help, using phrases like:

"John, Jane, and Jim, please stack the chairs in this half of the room — put them over by the bleachers. Make sure the stacks have no more than four chairs each."

"Sam, Sally, Sue, and Sarah, please stack the chairs in this half of the room over by the front door."

"Pete and Pat, please pick up any trash and put it in the bin."

"The rest of you — George, Paul, Veronica — put the costumes in the box and take the box to the dressing room."

Alternatively, you can put the group into "clean-up teams," and rotate the tasks each week. Team A can do chairs, Team B tables, Team C collect scripts, Team D pick up trash. This becomes easier as you become aware of the various tasks required to return the room back to its normal state, and how long each one takes.

While the group members are finishing their tasks, you can walk around and check for stray personal belongings and make sure that everyone is collecting their things. Use positive reinforcement, with phrases like "I see five people doing a great job clearing the props away," or "I see John and Joe are almost finished with stacking the chairs." If someone finishes his or her task early, he or she can either wait or — as an innovative gesture — help someone else. Perhaps ask them to double check that nothing is draped over the piano, stashed behind a chair, left on a windowsill, or left in the restroom.

Don't let anyone leave until everyone is ready to go. If necessary, stand by the door or assign a few of those already finished with their tasks to stand by the door. You may be tempted to bolt and lock the door, but your local fire department may frown on such a move.

To help make this vital portion of the session more interesting, try the following ideas:

- Use a timer to see who can do the tasks in the shortest amount of time.
- Count down out loud as the group works.
- See if they can complete all the tasks in the same time it takes to sing a particular show tune.
- Have a large paper with the tasks listed posted on the wall and check them off as they are completed.

Dividing the Group into Smaller Groups within the Workshop

It is inevitable that you will need to have your workshop group subdivide and work in smaller groups. Children, like everybody, will have their preferences about whom they want to work with. Whether you dictate who is in each group or leave the kids to choose for themselves is up to you. The kids will usually opt for self-selection, which has both advantages and disadvantages:

Advantages of self-selected groups

- A group who chooses its own members may be more relaxed and less inhibited, especially in scenes involving physical action and miming.
- Ideas may flow more freely and spark off each other more readily.
- New or shy members will tend to seek each other out and get to know each other at their own pace.
- Noisier, more extroverted children tend to gravitate toward each other, and must then share parts with each other. If they are assigned into separate groups, these children often dominate the proceedings and seize all the good roles.
- If a group of quiet children work together, they each tend to have a better chance of having their say and playing a lead character in a group scene.

Disadvantages of self-selected groups

- The announcement, "Get into a group of four or five" will always result in best friends grabbing each other and clinging together as if drowning at sea. Children who don't know anyone may feel isolated and lose confidence. However, if you

60

work to integrate new members into the group, this shouldn't present a problem. See the section, "Integrating New Members into the group" later in this chapter.

- Actors who work with the same people each week tend to become stale.
- The children may actually appreciate the chance to get to know other children better, but are so accustomed to their group patterns they don't know how to do this.
- Age groups, sexes, and races may not mix by choice. However, on-stage, people do work with people unlike themselves, so this gives your performers more opportunity to develop confidence in working with a variety of people.
- One group may always be stronger than the others, which can be demoralizing to the rest.
- Some groups may end up without an organizer who makes things happen, or without anyone creative and good at thinking up ideas.
- Some kids may be left out and will feel very uncomfortable about asking to join a group.

From a practical point of view, it is usually best to alternate how groups are formed over the course of the workshops. You take control of the group formation during some sessions and let the kids have free choice during other sessions. Just make it clear in the beginning that it is your prerogative to control group formation. If they ask why, explain that they need to work with all sorts of different performers to develop the widest variety of skills.

Tips for productive group work

If you are going to assign groups, it helps to make the assignment as random as possible. To achieve this, ask the kids to "number off" to the number of groups you wish to create. For example, if you want a group of twenty to form five smaller groups, ask each child in turn to call out "one," "two," "three," "four," "five," and then to start again with "one." Take a moment to make sure everyone remembers his or her number. Then clearly indicate where you want the different groups to work. For example, your instructions might be "All ones to the corner by the flag. All twos to the corner by the piano. All threes to the middle of the wall with the windows," and so forth.

Alternatively, you can ask them to call out letters (A, B, C, D, etc.), items (apples, peaches, pears) or even groups or properties connected with the show (orphans, millionaires, stray dogs, servants, radio announcers).

With self-selected groups, be sure to go around and make sure everyone has actually ended up in a group. Talk to any "strays" to see where they would prefer to be and try to get them into a group where they will be appreciated. Make sure everyone participates.

With either type of group, if you are concerned about "role hogging" within groups, reserve the right to assign parts within each group. You can use the same "number off" system as described above. Then you simply declare that all "ones" play Annie, all "twos" play Warbucks, or if you are concerned only about one or two players, simply walk up to the group and assign a smaller role to those actors who usually take the biggest one: "Jamie, I'd like you to play an extra urchin in this particular exercise."

Integrating New Members into the Group — Their First Session

Many new members join because they already know someone in the cast and are interested in being in the show. If a new member joins who doesn't know anyone in the group already, it is important that you develop a good relationship with that child and his or her parents. This relationship is fundamental to his or her liking the group and wanting to return. The interest you show in the child will boost the confidence the parents feel when meeting you. It will spur them to encourage the child to return and to lend help later.

If the parent has phoned in advance and you have time to send them a flyer and registration form, do so. Encourage the potential new member to arrive a few minutes early. This extra time will enable you to collect (or hand out) the flyer and registration form. More crucially, it will enable you to introduce yourself to the child and parents. Find out what name the child prefers to be called and how it is pronounced. Ask a few basic questions that will help you remember the child, such as if they live nearby, other interests they have, where they go to school, or who their favorite performer is.

By now, other kids have started to show up. Introduce the new one to two or three of them, and specifically assign one child to be the newcomer's "buddy" for the session. Instruct the buddy to help the newcomer to get to know the facility, such as where the restrooms are; include him or her into any group work if the group is self-selected; explain any procedures, such as the break and clearing up; and introduce as many other participants as possible. By meeting others as soon as possible, the newcomer can start choosing his or her own friends all the more quickly.

At the beginning of the session, introduce the newcomer to the entire group, perhaps including a few bits of the information you gleaned during your first encounter.

Chapter 5
Teaching Theatrical Basics

At some point early in the workshop series, you need to make sure all your actors have some understanding of the basic theatrical terms and techniques: stage areas, actor positions, stage business, and being visible to the audience. This knowledge will help you communicate with them about the show throughout the auditions and rehearsals. As time goes on, the group will gradually learn musical and other stage terminology. Usually the cast enjoys learning and using theatrical jargon.

Stage Areas

Teach the classic stage areas and their abbreviations. You may want to do this the first session or as soon as possible thereafter, as the schedule calls for the participants to start doing things on-stage by the third session.

The stage is divided into nine areas. *Center* is obvious; *left* and *right* are from the actors' point of view as they face the audience. *Up* is away from the audience; *down* is toward the audience. See figure 9. As the director, you will become accustomed to using "left" and "right" that contradicts how you are standing, which is facing the stage. If you get confused, just turn around and face away from the stage so your right and left matches that of your performers.

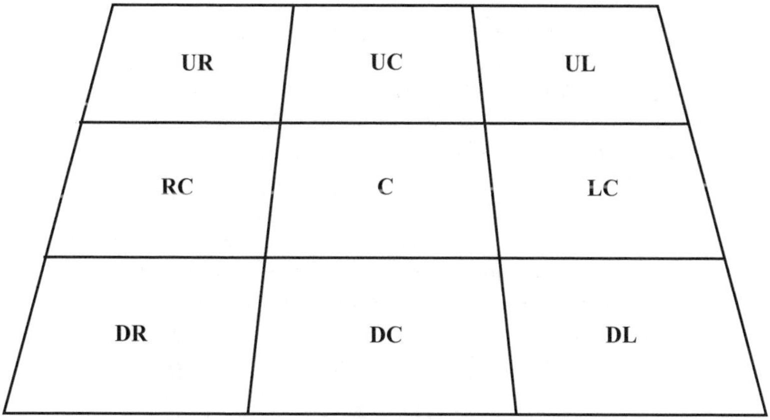

Audience
Figure 9 – Stage areas

Stage Areas Game — Upstage/Downstage

To help the performers learn the different stage areas and follow instructions to move to them, try the following Upstage/Downstage game. In the U.K., many youngsters know the game "Port Starboard," especially if they have been in the Brownies or Cubs. We invented this game as a variation on that theme.

Objective: To learn the names for the positions of the nine main areas of a stage.

First, as a reminder, demonstrate where the nine stage areas are by walking to each of them, or asking a performer to walk to each of them as you call them out. Remind them that "left" and "right" are from the actor's point of view as he or she directly faces the audience.

Directions:
1. All performers stand in a group in the middle of the stage area.
2. If playing for the first time, explain the rules. You will now shout out either a stage area, for example, "Down stage left!" or the instruction "Freeze."
3. If you call out a stage area, all performers must run to that area. The last one to arrive there is out and must leave the stage.

4. If you shout "Freeze," no one can move until you shout "Un-freeze." You may actually shout a stage area in between. Anyone who moves before you shout "Un-freeze" is out and must leave the stage. This helps them stay attentive and helps keep the game short.

5. At the start of the game, just to warm up, allow a few practice tries in which no one gets out.

6. Play the game for real, calling out different stage areas or "Freeze" each time. Sometimes call out the area they are already in. Anyone who takes a few steps is out.

7. Those that are out join you in the audience area. They can write down stage areas on pieces of paper and pass them to you for shouting out. You can also assign them to call out the stage directions, although you must clearly inform the players on the stage of the new leader.

8. For fun add mimes. Ask the group to run to a stage area and, for example, rig the lights, build scenery, put on makeup, or stroke the theatre cat. You can also ask them to get into "dressing rooms" of threes or fours. Anyone left over is out. Our personal favorite is to call out "Director's coming" and they all have to stand up straight and salute!

9. Continue until there is only one performer left. This person is the winner.

Actor Positions

It is also helpful if you and the actors know the terminology for how to stand on-stage. This shared knowledge helps you communicate and clarify *how* they should stand or sit on-stage, not just *where*. Again, left and right are from the actors' point of view as they face the audience. See figure 10.

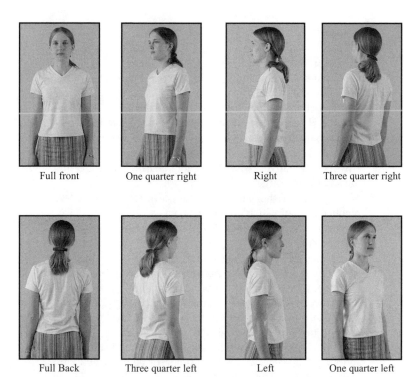

| Full front | One quarter right | Right | Three quarter right |

| Full Back | Three quarter left | Left | One quarter left |

Figure 10 – Actor positions

Actor Positions Game

You can play a game, similar to the preceding Upstage/ Downstage game, to reinforce the lesson on actors' positions. For greater variation and challenge, once the actors become familiar with the terminology, you can combine stage areas with actor positions.

Objective: To learn the names for the body positions or stances actors take on-stage.

First, as a reminder, you or an actor demonstrates the main body positions. Remind them that "left" and "right" are from the actor's point of view as he or she directly faces the audience.

Directions:
1. All performers stand in a line in the middle of the stage area.
2. If playing for the first time, explain the rules. You will now shout out either a position, for example, "Full back," or the instruction "Freeze."
3. If you call out a position, all performers must take that position. The last one do so is out and must leave the stage.
4. If you shout "Freeze," no one can move until you shout "Un-freeze." You may actually shout a position in between. Anyone who moves before you shout "Un-freeze" is out and must leave the stage.
5. At the start of the game, just to warm up, allow a few practice tries in which no one gets out.
6. Now start the game for real. Call out either different actor positions or "Freeze."
7. Those that are out join you in the audience area. They can write down different actor positions on pieces of paper and hand them to you for calling out. You can also assign one of them to call out the stage directions, although you must clearly inform the players on the stage of the new leader.
8. As with the Upstage/Downstage game, you can add mimes for variety. Ask the group to take a position and study their scripts, paint scenery, comb their hair, or be paralyzed with fear of the theater ghost. You can also ask them to sit, lie down, crouch over, or reach up. Or add a stage direction: "Walk to downstage right and turn full back."
9. Continue until there is only one performer left. This person is the winner.

Stage Business

As you begin rehearsals, encourage your group to think about developing appropriate stage business for their characters. You can introduce this idea in the course of rehearsals, or you can devote a short session to it, with an exercise to help them create interesting stage business.

Stage business or simply *business* refers to a character's actions that help to underline the character's personality or mood. Stage business can continue as a background to dialog and helps create more interesting scenes or characters. It also helps give the actors something to do with their hands.

Some examples are:
- Two of the gangsters in *Guys and Dolls* arm-wrestling or tossing a football around while conversing.
- Tallulah filing her nails while Fat Sam is on the telephone (*Bugsy Malone*).
- Guppy, the cleaner, mopping the floor; Junior polishing his sheriff's star (*Phantom of the Op'ry*).
- Joseph drawing hieroglyphics in his cell (*Joseph and the Amazing Technicolor Dreamcoat*).
- Dodger eating an apple (*Oliver*).

If used unchecked, stage business can distract the audience and upstage the main action of the scene. Used sensibly, it adds interest and texture to a scene and gives those with minor roles something to create and develop.

Stage business game

This game is similar to Upstage/Downstage and it builds on the knowledge of stage areas and actor positions, as well as introduces ideas for stage business.

Objective: To try out different ideas for stage business; to reinforce knowledge of stage terminology.

First, ask your actors to recall terminology already learned, that is, stage areas and actor positions.

Directions:
1. All performers stand in a line in the middle of the stage area.
2. If playing for the first time, explain the rules. You will now shout out either a set of instructions to carry out some stage business or the command, "Freeze." The stage business instruction may specify a stage area to go to or an actor stance to take.
3. If you call out an instruction for stage business, all performers must perform the stage business, moving to any particular area or taking any stance specified. The last one to do so is out and must leave the stage. For example you may instruct them to "Drink hot coffee and spill it," or give

more elaborate detail such as, "Sit down and flip through a magazine," or "Take three steps downstage right and nail up a sign."

4. If you shout "Freeze," no one can move until you shout "Un-freeze." You may actually shout another instruction in between. Anyone who moves before you shout "Un-freeze" is out and must leave the stage.

5. At the start of the game, just to warm up, allow a few practice tries in which no one gets out.

6. Start the real game, calling out different examples of stage business or "Freeze" each time.

7. Those that are out join you in the audience area. They can write down examples of stage business on pieces of paper and hand them to you to shout out.

8. Continue until there is only one performer left. This person is the winner.

Helping Actors to Be More Visible On-stage

During performances, audiences long to see those they know in the show as much and as clearly as possible. Actors can help themselves to be seen by employing the following tactics:

• Use upstage arms for gestures when possible so faces won't be blocked.

• Angle the feet so that the downstage leg doesn't cross in front of the upstage leg, which causes the body to turn upstage and be less visible.

• Unless in a highly confrontational or romantic scene, actors should try to stand at angles to each other and not face to face. This makes more of their bodies and faces visible to the audience.

Sometimes these adjustments are known as *cheating out*. The actors' facial expressions are also easier to see if they:

• Keep hair out of their eyes. The kids may profess to loathe brushing and pinning their hair back, but unseen eyes mean an unseen actor.

• Speak loudly and clearly. A good strong voice automatically draws attention to its producer.

Stage Visibility Game

For this game, have the kids improvise a short scene from the play, or any typical daily scene, such as gossiping around their lockers or having lunch. They first act it out trying to be as invisible as possible to the audience. The second time, they try to be as visible as possible, using all the tactics listed above.

Other Theatrical Terms

As the sessions progress, you will naturally start introducing and using various theatrical and musical terms such as mime, callboy, chorus, or libretto. For a list of commonly used theatrical and musical terms, see Appendix 1 – "Glossary of Theatrical and Musical Terms."

Teach and reinforce the correct use of these terms by explaining what it means each time you use it. For example, you may say, "Mary is going to prompt at this rehearsal. If you forget a line, stay quiet, stay in character, and she will read out the beginning of the line to *prompt* you," or "Everyone come out now and sit on the apron of the stage. Come sit on its edge toward the audience, which is called the *apron*."

Chapter 6

Introducing Your Chosen Musical to the Group (1 Session)

Now that you have decided on a show, you need to introduce it to your group. Although you may give a brief overview of the musical at the first session, presenting a more careful, planned introduction to the show helps the actors to become familiar with the entire story, hear all the songs, get to know the entire cast of characters, and become enthusiastic about it.

It is this enthusiasm that will propel everyone through the occasional low points of producing a show — the rehearsal that seems to go nowhere, the loss of your lighting technician to the football season, or a leading man who seems unable to learn his lines.

The introduction usually takes place during the workshop before the audition sessions begin and requires about two hours if you plan to show a video, less time if you do not. This book assumes that everyone in your group, club, or class will be part of the final show, no matter what role they each actually have. In this case, the auditions do not function as a "knock out" process.

However, you may be in a position where you need to hold tryouts to form a reasonably sized group, committed to producing the show. This might occur because your group would otherwise be far too big and unwieldy, or some kids may not consider being involved unless they win a large role. You can still adapt our suggestions to an introduction to the musical. In this case, you have a choice: you can present the introduction as a pre-tryout session to build interest in the show, or you can run the introduction as your first session with the chosen cast.

We recommend running the introductory session *before* tryouts. Sometimes young would-be performers have preconceived ideas about which roles they want and don't understand the breadth of possibilities open to them in other parts, and it saves you having to explain repeatedly the different roles in the show.

In introducing the show to the group, we advise that you avoid the inclination to ask the group to sit and "read through" the play. This tradition tends to be stultifying to young performers. It is almost impossible to "read through" a large chorus number or dance scene, and those are the scenes you need your group to be the most interested in and most enthusiastic about. If there are only a few major speaking roles, only the main characters will have much to do during a read-through, and the rest of the group will become restless.

Introducing the Show with a Video Version

Once you have decided on your musical, it is worthwhile to rent or buy a video version, if it is available, to show the group. Sometimes more than one version may be available. Plan on spending at least two hours watching and discussing the video.

Problems and benefits of showing a video version

Some group leaders may be reluctant to show a video because they feel it may stifle creativity within the group or demoralize the group with a high, and impossible to duplicate, display of professionalism. They may be concerned that if the performers see the video version, they will simply try to copy its actors' performances.

We have found the benefits outweigh any drawbacks. Since you will be showing the video only once, quite early in the sessions and before any casting has taken place, it is unlikely anyone in your group will remember any performance well enough to copy it. Realistically, your group will probably not surpass a professional production costing millions to produce. But watching one gives them something to aim for and learn from.

A related problem that can occur with the group watching any video version is that they expect the plot, props, and other details of their own show will be a carbon copy of the film version they have just seen. For example, after watching *Oliver* or *Annie*, you will always hear the question, "Will we have a real dog?"

Replicating the film version is; of course, impossible for many reasons: no production is the same, films by definition are different from live performances; the junior version you are producing may have different dialog or songs from the adult film version; and the stage script itself is often different from the film script. For example, Bull's-eye, the dog in the film version of *Oliver*, is not in the stage version; it was simply written into the film version.

Therefore, before you start to play the video, stress to your group that what they are about to see is *not* the script they will perform. However, be prepared throughout the rehearsals to hear, ad infinitum, the immortal words, "In the film … ." Simply be prepared to repeat, ad infinitum, your own immortal response: "We're not doing the film."

In general, watching a film version of the show helps the performers in the following tasks:

Identifying the show

Your performers may never have heard of the show, no matter how familiar you are with it or how famous it may seem to be. It's very hard to become enthusiastic about something unknown. By watching the video, your performers will become acquainted with what they will actually be doing. They will be able to visualize the scenes and setting.

Learning the story

Musicals usually have multiple characters, locations, plots, and subplots. The performers will be more interested in the show if they understand the entire story, and watching the video helps achieve this.

It can be very difficult to pick up the actual story from reading the script cold. Sometimes the plot can turn on a single action or line that can be easily missed. For example, in *Guys and Dolls*, Nathan Detroit's bet that Sky Masterson will be unable to convince Miss Sarah to go away to Havana is the crux of the plot, but it is easy to miss it from reading the play because Nathan's choice of Miss Sarah is partially mimed and not actually part of the dialog.

Understanding the characters

By watching the show, the performers easily learn to identify who the main characters are and start to think about what character they would like to play. It also helps them to develop a sense of character traits, such as age, accent, idiosyncrasies, profession, interests, and wardrobe, and to see the relationships between characters.

Appreciating the context

Musicals are usually set in places and times different from the contemporary scene of your performers. Nineteenth-century London or Russia and 1930s New York or Chicago are a long way mentally from where your group is. Youngsters often think Grease is set in the 1970s, the decade of its release, although its actual setting is 1950s. Most video versions of the musicals make some attempt to evoke the historical context, local setting, typical objects, and period costumes. Knowledge of the show's context helps your group understand the story more fully while throwing a short history lesson into the bargain.

Making a transition from the last show

If your group has just finished performing a show, they might experience a sense of post-production blues and instant nostalgia. They may have fallen in love with their parts and their scenes and profess to have forgotten what they did before they were part of that show. By showing the video, you help them to focus on the future and what they will be doing next.

Running the viewing session

Planning the session

For this session, try to arrange the use of a video player and a television with a screen large enough for the group to watch the show comfortably. Check the location of the power outlet and bring an extension cord if necessary. Before the session, test the equipment and make sure the video, cables, and other components are all compatible. Check that the video is fully rewound.

For the group to gain the most benefit from watching the video, take time to structure the viewing session. You cannot simply settle your performers in front of the TV screen and put your feet up for ninety minutes.

Introducing the video

Before you begin showing the video, start out by asking a few questions:

- Has anyone seen this show before? Live production or video? What did you think of it?
- Who can tell us where the story takes place? Has anyone

visited that part of the world (assuming it is a real geographic area)?

• Does anyone know what time period this story takes place in? What do we know about that time period?

• Does anyone know the names of some of the main characters? Who are they?

• Does anyone know any songs from the show? What are they?

Depending on the answers, you can supply further information. Keep this introduction short, about five minutes, depending on how much prior knowledge the group has to share.

At this point, write the names of the main characters down on a blackboard, whiteboard, or flipchart along with their major characteristics ("old," "easily frightened," "loves money") and the relations between the characters ("his girlfriend," "her mother"). You can then point to the names as the characters are first seen in the video. Sometimes it is baffling to figure out who is who.

If you have them available, supply the group with song sheets or scripts. They enjoy singing along with the big famous numbers or following along with the dialog.

Then ask the group to think about the following as they watch the video:

• What characters — major or minor — could they see themselves playing?

• How is the setting different from where they live?

• How is the time period different from their own?

• What are the main action points and moods of the show?

During the video viewing

As your group watches the video, stay attentive and do the following:

Explain key actions. Pause the video if some action crucial to the plot takes place or important background information is given. When pivotal action happens so quickly it is missed or background information is tossed away in a line, subsequent developments can seem mystifying and illogical. Questions like "What did X just do/see/hear?" or "What did you just learn?" or "Why is this important?" help the group learn the plot. If necessary, you can briefly explain, "This is important because ..."

Ward off restlessness. If a big number comes up, such as "Consider Yourself" from *Oliver* or "It's a Hard Knock Life for Us" from *Annie*, that the entire group will be doing, tell them so and encourage them to sing along. By singing along yourself, you will find they all join in.

If you know a particular song or scene in the video will not be in your production, such as "Adelaide, Adelaide, Ever-loving Adelaide" in *Guys and Dolls*, skip it entirely.

For most solos and duets, just play the first four to five lines, unless it is a blockbuster like "Tomorrow" from *Annie*. Fast-forward through the rest while you explain briefly what the song is about. For instance say, "In this song, Joseph sings about how he will not be too depressed by being in jail and his own life is not what is most important."

You may find your group becoming restless during some of the dialog scenes, particularly romantic scenes. If this is the case, be prepared to fast-forward through the scene while you explain salient points of the action: "Sky and Sarah seem to fall in love in this scene."

After the video finishes

After the video, go back to the questions you asked them to think about before they began watching. Encourage as much participation as possible.

- Which characters did you see that you would like to play? Think about at least one major role and a couple of secondary or minor roles.
- Who were some characters that were not on stage very long that seemed interesting or challenging?
- How would you describe each of the different characters?
- What did you learn about the historical background?
- What did you learn about the physical setting of the play?
- Are there different "groups" in the play? How are they different from each other? Which group do you see yourself in?

Finally, remind them — the first of many times — "We're not doing the film." If you have extra time, run the dance routine you taught at the first session, just to get everyone moving after sitting for so long.

Introducing the Show without Using a Video

Although the video is a convenient way to introduce the show, not all musicals have a version available on video. However, you still need to introduce the show, the plot, and the characters, and build excitement and interest with your group.

Almost all musicals have a CD or audiotape version of the music available as well as an instrumental acompaniment track. For some royalty plays, the soundtrack may only be available from the New York Broadway or London West End production.

If a CD, audiotape, or soundtrack is available, you can follow many of the same steps used in viewing the video, making some adjustments for not having anything to see. If you have a chalk or white board available, put the names of the major characters on the board, and draw stick figures with a semblance of costume on them.

Hand out song sheets or scripts. Describe the characters and action of each scene in order, being as vivid and brief as you possibly can. Play a recorded version of the songs as they occur in the action. Ask them to sing along with all the songs in the show. Be sure to join in the singing yourself. After you have finished describing the action and playing the songs, ask the same sort of questions you would after viewing the video.

This process may not take as long as watching a video. Use the extra time for auditions and the rehearsals — never a bad idea.

Chapter 7

Casting the Show

Considerations in Casting the Show

Your knowledge of the group

In each group you work with, you will see a wide range of aptitude, attitude, and application, with most participants having an uneven mixture of the three. From your viewpoint, you run the group to improve the skills of the individuals and to provide an enjoyable and interesting experience for both them and their audience. Hopefully, they come to the sessions with a positive attitude and willingness to try to learn and take direction.

If you are putting together an entirely new group and don't know their skills or potential very well, consider extending the audition period by a few sessions. The group can still begin learning the dance routines and songs, and you will have more time to judge how well each performer can handle the roles.

If you have a well-established group, you may already have some ideas of who will play which role. However, you still need to be open-minded and receptive to what new members have to offer. Kids develop and change quickly. Your main dilemma may be whether to reward loyalty and hard work or to cast strictly on the basis of talent.

Choosing between talent and hard work

Your group members have very little control over what talent they have, but they can often make up for it with work and dedication. Many improve with time and practice, gaining confidence, poise, and control. This is what they are here for — to learn. It is most rewarding when someone who started with the group as a shy, unconfident chorus member stands up and sings a solo.

However, in the hard task of casting your chosen musical from your particular group, you may have extremes to choose from: very talented people who are unreliable in attending rehearsals or cannot memorize lines; loyal, hardworking children who may not have the talent to sustain a *major* character; and the rare find, someone talented and hardworking! As a group leader you make your own decisions about how much you will overlook occasional poor behavior in return for exquisitely sung songs, or how much you are willing to overlook weak characterization to help reward a loyal participant. Hopefully, your chosen script can accommodate what talent your group has to offer, and enable as many children as possible to have interesting, challenging parts.

If your group has been working together for a while, or even if it is a relatively new group, it can be helpful to discuss these difficult decisions openly with the kids. Explain you have to decide whether to reward the long service and loyalty of those who have been attending for a while or to draw on the obvious talents of a newcomer. You are debating whether to cast the same, highly talented actors *again* this year for the leading roles because they are so suited for the roles and will do them easily, or to use hardworking chorus members who have potential to be developed if given a chance. During the auditions, you may want to try playing the game, "Who would you cast?" which is discussed in detail at the end of this chapter.

Casting each performer to be a star

Obviously, some performers will wind up with major roles. However, we have found it increases your satisfaction as a director, makes the children happy, and pleases the parents if you plan the show's performance so that *all* cast members have a chance to show off some of their talent, particularly if their talent may be overlooked or unexpected. Because the audition period is fairly lengthy, you will have many opportunities to see talent, and to start planning how to put each person — if only for a few seconds — in the limelight.

As you work through the auditions and observe your group, think how each could have at least one glorious moment, however brief, that is his or hers alone and no one else's. Ponder possibilities such as saying a minor character's one line with great aplomb, making a funny face, performing a stunt, taking a small role, singing a solo line in a chorus song, or making a solo movement in a group dance. At that moment, the actor should feel he or she is an individual absolutely essential to the show's drama and delight.

For example, the pub landlord in *Oliver* who announces Nancy's song is the unequalled star of that particular moment. Consider adjusting stage action to allow a specific cast member to bask in the limelight. The script of *Annie* calls for the character Molly, who is already a strong role, to end up in the laundry basket. Why not assign one of your smaller, less confident actors be the little one in the basket? Check what minor adjustments your licensing arrangements allow.

Another way of involving a range of talents and recognizing effort in your group is to give some chorus performers important stage crew duties. See the section, "Planning and Rehearsing Scene Changes" in chapter 14.

Working around vocal issues

Singing ability is the most decisive factor in casting a musical. To complicate matters further, unless your cast members are already singing in a choir somewhere or taking voice lessons, you will be working with untrained voices and ears. There are so many other demands in putting together a musical that you — or your musical director — will not have much time to train these voices and ears, so you usually need to rely largely on natural ability in casting major singing roles.

Sometimes you will find the perfect performer for a character — except for the voice. If you want to cast that actor in a role, here are some possible solutions to divert attention from the performer's vocal weaknesses:

- Can the character's song(s) be "spoken" rather than sung?
- Can the character's song(s) be cut?
- Can another character sing along? For example, Tiny Tim in *Scrooge* could be joined by one of his siblings in "Beautiful Winter's Morning."
- Can the song be sung by another character? For example, in *Guys and Dolls,* "Sit Down, You're Rocking the Boat" could be sung by an unnamed gangster, not necessarily Nicely-Nicely Johnson.

Both of the last two options enable you to put the spotlight on good vocalists who may be weak on acting or are unsuited to the actual role. Also, if an actor who has had leading parts in previous shows is taking a smaller role in this play, he or she will appreciate a chance to shine once again as a solo performer.

Most license arrangements will allow reassigning songs, but double-check with your publisher.

Planning and Running Audition Sessions (4–6 Sessions)

The primary purpose of the audition sessions is, of course, to cast all the roles in the play and to give as many people as much time on-stage as possible. Our approach assumes that everyone in the group will, at the very least, be in many chorus scenes and have a chance to shine as an individual at least once in the show. Actors playing leading roles can sing in the chorus in scenes where their characters don't appear and when they do not have complicated costume changes backstage.

The audition process outlined here does not ask anyone to stand up on stage and read a script cold. It does not require anyone to line up outside a room waiting to do a prepared scene that could be interrupted at any time with the blood-curdling cry of "Next!" Our approach to auditions serves to familiarize the group with the show and to give you ideas for characterization and choreography: in short, to begin rehearsing.

The auditions are a continual process, incorporated into the normal workshop activities of the group, and usually take four to six two-hour sessions to complete. As a general rule, out of twelve hours total, you will need two hours for dancing, four hours for singing and six hours for acting. To make the sessions more varied, try to keep to the ratio but mix up acting, singing, and dance auditions within a single session.

If you don't have a video of the play for the kids to watch, you can start audition activities a bit earlier. Also, if the group is newly formed, try to extend the auditions for as long as possible until you are satisfied you have seen everyone as fully and fairly as possible. Because the auditions involve learning musical numbers from the show, they actually function as rehearsals, so little time is wasted.

There are several advantages to spreading auditions out over several sessions and making them seem like regular workshops:

• You allow those who miss a session due to other commitments or illness or who just have an out-of-sorts day not to feel they have missed a chance to get a part — they know they have had several opportunities to shine.

• Several sessions present you more chances to see actors perform as individuals, as well as part of a pair or part of a group. You do not need to base a decision on seeing someone read a particular role only once or twice.

• You have many opportunities to see the children perform in both large and small roles, which gives you ideas of how you can highlight each actor's talent in the actual show.

• Often people are quite disappointed if they don't get the role they especially want, and they may drop out of the production because they don't want to be "just in the chorus." This is a shame, because those very actors could, with some experience, become prime candidates for larger roles later on. If your actors invest time in the audition process, and if they find it interesting, instructive, and fun, they may well become hooked on performing the show, no matter how large or small a part they actually play.

• The auditions function as rehearsals because they involve learning songs and dance numbers and improvising the action.

• A longer audition period gives you more time to get to know the group as a whole and for the group members to get to know each other without the pressure (yet) of preparing to perform the show.

In fact, your performers may get so caught up in the audition activities that they forget they are actually auditioning. It is important to announce when the audition sessions will officially start, for example, "The next five sessions, that is the rest of September and the first two weeks in October, will be audition sessions. By October 20, I plan to announce the final cast of the show." Mention at the beginning and end of each session that an audition is taking place that day so everyone will know that the workshops are functioning as auditions.

Sample audition session structure

Not every audition will be the same, but the sample structure outlined in the following paragraphs may give you ideas for planning the sessions. Times and activities will vary. For example, one of the acting auditions may be of prepared scenes instead of improvisations based on action from a scene. If your musical director can come to only one audition, make sure that it is the one where the kids do their individual songs and that you do as much singing as possible. The same holds true for dancing if you have a separate choreographer who can only attend a single session.

See sessions 3–6 in the sample thiry-six-week rehearsal schedule for a breakdown of each audition.

Administrative matters (10 minutes)

Take attendance, collect any fees, and explain the purpose of the day, which is to start to learn the show and to audition for parts. If you are passing out scripts that the cast will keep for the remainder of the rehearsal period, allow extra time. Pass out song sheets if you are using them.

Learn a song (20 minutes)

To warm up your performers' voices and get them into the mood of the show, direct the entire group to go through one of the show's big singing numbers that you have already introduced in an earlier session, such as "It's a Hard Knock Life" from *Annie* or the title song from *Is There a Doctor in the House?* Use recorded or live music for accompaniment.

Then following your rehearsal plan, teach the next song in the show. If you don't feel you have enough time to teach the entire song, teach a few stanzas. The purpose is to provide the kids with some lyrics to sing for their singing auditions. See the section, "Singing," in chapter 10 for guidance on how to teach songs. If your performers have learned the dance movements of the song in previous sessions, ask them to do the movements as well as sing. Otherwise, they can sit or stand and sing the songs.

Learn a dance (40 minutes)

Teach a dance routine to one of the songs you have learned. If you do not have time to teach the entire dance, just concentrate on one or two verses. The purpose is to provide something for the kids to perform in their dance audition. For ideas on developing and teaching dance sequences, see the section, "Choreography," in chapter 10.

Explain acting improvisation and assign groups (5 minutes)
Give a scenario from the show for the acting improvisation,
explaining the characters and the basic action of the scene. See the
following section, "Acting auditions," for details of how to run
these.

Break (10 minutes)
During the break, the performers can work in groups and start
planning their improvisations.

Acting audition (25 minutes)
In groups, the actors perform their improvisations. See the
following section, "Acting auditions," for details on how to evaluate
acting potential.

Singing audition (10 minutes)
Sing any songs the performers have learned. Allow performers
to sing stanzas on their own or in small groups. See the section,
"Singing auditions" later in this chapter for suggestions on how to
run these and what to look for in judging singing potential.

Clearing up (5 minutes)
Remind actors that an audition has been taking place and tell
them about any that might be remaining.

Acting auditions

Improvised scenes
Your performers do not need scripts for improvised scenes. The
group improvises scenes based on your description of the action and
characters in a scene from the show. The performers should already
be familiar with the storyline and characters, either from watching
and discussing the video or from listening to the soundtrack and
hearing your description of the plot and characters.

Before running improvisation auditions, complete the
following:

• Pick out a strong "acting" scene in the play, that is, a scene
  with mostly dialog, no singing, and with at least four to six
  characters. Try to find scenes for all the leading characters.
  Usually, the first scene in which you see the characters you are
  auditioning is a good choice.

• Prepare a short summary of the scene's action points and
  descriptions of the characters. Go through the action point by
  point. See figure 11 for a sample summary from *Annie*.

Generally, you will work on one scene per audition session, so if you have three scenes selected, you will use each of them once during three audition sessions.

Action Points: Opening bedroom scene — *Annie*

Characters: Annie, Molly, Pepper, Miss Hannigan, Mr. Bundles, other orphans

1. Orphans are asleep.
2. One (Molly) has a nightmare and starts screaming.
3. All the others wake up.
4. Another (Pepper) threatens to beat her if she doesn't stop.
5. Annie comforts Molly. Molly goes back to sleep and everyone else does too.
6. Annie, who has only been pretending to go back to sleep, gets up, packs her bag, and tries to escape from the orphanage (actors choose how this is done).
7. Miss Hannigan comes in and catches her. She gives her a wallop with a hairbrush ("the paddle").
8. Miss Hannigan punishes them all by making them get up and scrub the floor and strip the beds.
9. Annie hides in a basket.
10. Mr. Bundles comes in for the laundry pickup and wheels Annie away.
11. Miss Hannigan comes back and takes roll. She discovers Annie is missing and becomes livid. She runs off after Mr. Bundles.
12. Orphans cheer.

Figure 11 – Sample summary of action points

When you are ready to run an improvised acting audition, take the following steps:

- Put your performers into groups according to the number of characters in the scene. If the scene has four characters, put together groups of four. *Don't* worry about matching the sex of the characters to the actors in the groups.
- Explain the scene and characters. Ask each group to decide which parts each member will play and give them some time to prepare to act out the scene you have described. They can work over the break as well as having some time during the session.
- Give the groups a clear, set amount of time for preparation and be ready to watch any spare chair, table, or stray costume be

drafted into some use for the scene. Usually twenty minutes is sufficient rehearsal time. If the groups start to get restless before the allocated time is up, bring the rehearsal time to an earlier close. Otherwise, five minutes before the end of the rehearsal time, start warning them, "five more minutes!" ... "three more minutes!" and so on.

- The groups can use the stage to present their scene, if you have a stage, or they can just act out the scene in a space where others can easily see them.
- Each group then presents the scene.
- As the improvisations are being performed, allow the groups to present them enough times so that everyone gets a chance to play the role he or she particularly wants. This means that each group might present their scene several times, each time with individuals playing different characters. So, if you have seven groups of three playing a scene with Annie, Warbucks, and Grace, you may well see twenty-one Annies, twenty-one Warbucks, and twenty-one Graces! In this way, every group member gets a chance to play a big role — even if for a short time — and no one can complain later that he or she did not have a chance to try out for a big part.
- At the same time, make sure that any actor you have mentally short-listed for a specific part actually auditions for that part.

As groups work to prepare their scenes, wander around and observe how they are getting on; such observation gives you additional chances to see who is seems to fit most successfully into certain roles. If you feel as if you are running short of time, and cannot really see all twenty-one Annies, twenty-one Warbucks, etc., insist — as subtly as possible — that certain performers take particular roles during their presentation. Hopefully, you can come back to any missed presentations at a time later in the audition sessions.

As you watch each scene, look at the individuals performing the scene as closely as possible. Ask yourself the following questions. Does the actor:

- Speak loudly enough?
- Enunciate words clearly?
- Speak with animation and expression? (If an accent is required for the part, is it attempted with any success?)

- Seem to understand what is happening in the scene?
- Seem to understand his or her relationship to other characters in the scene?
- Know where the audience is?
- Stay "in character" even if not speaking?
- Keep the dialog and energy going whatever happens?

Generally, improvising a single scene with strong characters will give you enough examples of raw talent to cast the show. However, if you have time, you can draw on a second or third scene with different characters as the basis of an improvisation. For example, you may want to ask the actors to improvise the scene from *Annie* that involves Warbucks and the President. This approach enables you to see a wider range of characters auditioned. Another way to see more characters is to use prepared scenes as described in the following section.

Other types of acting auditions

In addition to the improvised auditions outlined above, you can include slightly more formal auditions in which the performers use scripts or present prepared scenes. Here are some suggestions:

Sight-reading of scenes. The performers read through scenes you have chosen. These sessions can give you some ideas about voice projection and characterization, but they tend to be boring for the rest of the group to watch.

Prepared portions of solo/duet/small-group scenes. Performers who want to audition for leading roles, such as the eponymous Oliver, Annie, Bugsy Malone, Joseph, or Phantom of the Op'ry, can take the scripts home and memorize and present their part of a solo scene or a scene with just one or two other characters the following week. If you have many actors wanting to audition for several roles, this approach can take hours to get through. However, because you will need other actors to read in the other parts in these scenes, you will have an opportunity to see how a number of actors might handle other characters. Therefore, you can try out the Artful Dodger along with Oliver, Warbucks along with Annie, or Christine along with the Phantom.

Prepared group scenes. As an alternative, choose short scenes that have two to four players, focusing on the leads you want to audition. Appoint groups to memorize and present each scene the following week; if you want someone specifically to read a role,

88

here is your chance to assign it. Group members take the scripts home and learn their lines. At the beginning of the next session, allow a few minutes for groups to run through their scenes and ask them to perform the scenes in front of the group. Except for a short singing warm-up, this exercise needs to be the first activity of the session, because the performers will be nervous and not able to concentrate on much else.

Singing auditions

It is critical that singing auditions be structured and conducted so you hear singers individually. Most performers are more relaxed during the first singing audition session if they start by singing in a group and then sing single stanzas on their own in what would otherwise be a group musical number. Later, give the opportunity to those interested in auditioning for a lead role to sing a prepared solo.

If you have a separate musical director, try to arrange for him or her to attend one or more of the singing auditions, because they will probably be working more closely with the singers than you will. If the musical director can attend only one audition, make sure it is the one in which your performers sing their prepared solos or other pieces.

Running singing auditions

- Hand out scripts or song sheets (typed sheets with lyrics from all the songs) to the group. It is helpful if the stanzas are numbered.
- Cue up the tape or CD player; then have your performers sing through your chosen songs as a group, accompanied by the tape or CD. Insist they all sing the songs, even if you have, for audition purposes, chosen solo and duets as well as chorus numbers.
- If the group has been facing you, ask them to rearrange themselves so they face each other. They can arrange themselves in a single circle or in rows as space allows.
- Next put the performers into groups, perhaps five in each group. Then sing through some solos, duets, and chorus numbers again, but this time have each group sing a stanza in turn. This accustoms them to singing and listening to each other and helps them relax about performing in front of their peers.

89

- Find out which performers want to audition for parts that require solo songs. During the next rounds of singing, give each of these players a chance to sing a solo. Make sure to give anyone you think might be good in a singing role an opportunity to sing alone; try to choose a song of the character you would most like them to play.
- If someone is adamantly against singing alone, do not insist that they do. The player may become more confident during the auditions and want to try later on.
- Continue allocating stanzas or even a few lines to individuals who want to sing solo until you have heard them all, ideally a couple of times each audition. This method is certainly quicker than hearing twenty-eight people each sing an entire solo.
- For variety and fun, ask the groups to sing songs against type or out of character. For example, have a group of boys sing the "Hot Box Girls" number in *Guys and Dolls*.

During these sessions, observe the following about each singer. Does the singer:

- Keep in tune?
- Need to shriek or strain to hit high notes, or miss them completely?
- Sing with confidence and expression?
- Seem to know what the song expresses?
- Sing loudly enough? (We recommend that you use microphones for solo and duet numbers during the performance, but the singer needs to achieve some degree of volume without amplification.)

Movement and dance auditions

These auditions must show you two skills: whether the performer can a) follow and mimic dance steps and b) remember and perform an entire dance. The easiest and most efficient way for you or your choreographer to judge these two skills is to first teach the entire group a dance number from the show itself and then watch them perform it. It is also helpful to assign a short activity in which they develop and perform their own dance steps for one of the show numbers. This gives you a glimpse of any natural ability, shows you the type of moves they are comfortable doing, and usually provides some ideas for choreography.

90

Learning and performing a dance routine

For ideas on teaching dance routines, see the section, "Choreography," in chapter 10. Generally, during the six audition sessions you should aim to teach at least two or three routines. Once the group knows

Students develop their own choreography during dance auditions.

the routine, ask them to perform it in groups of five to six. As they perform, observe the following about each dancer. Does the dancer:

• Remember the routine?
• Follow the rhythm of the piece?
• Fit the moves in time to the music?
• Use his or her head and arms as well as his or her feet?
• Have facial expressions and *smile*?
• Capture the style of the movement?
• Appear confident in what he or she is doing?
• Seem coordinated in what he or she is doing?

Finally, who is copying whom?

Devising a group dance routine

An excellent audition variation is to divide the group into teams of six to eight people. Ask each group to create their own dance routine to the chorus stanza and at least one individual stanza of a dance number from the show. Play the song a couple of times through while they all listen. Then give them fifteen to twenty minutes to work out a dance. They can simply sing the song themselves while they are rehearsing in groups. If a group works quickly, members can go on to do more verses.

This audition exercise will not only give you a good sense of who can move well, but it will also give you ideas for dance movements and routines that the performers can actually do themselves. In watching the performances of these original dances, ask yourself the same questions as listed above under "Learning and performing a dance routine." As with the acting auditions, wander around and see how groups are progressing with the dance moves.

Helping the Group Understand Casting Decisions

Sometimes it is helpful to discuss casting issues, particularly if you are working with a long-established group. You can also use the following activity with newly formed groups to give them some experience in thinking about the entire show and making directorial decisions. The activity may also help individual performers accept disappointment when they do not get the role they wanted.

Who Would You Cast? Game

During one of the audition sessions, usually the last, distribute to each group member a list of the show's characters titled, "Who would you cast?" You may wish to format it as a three-columed table. In the first column, list each role to be cast. In the second, provide space for performers to write whom they would suggest for each role. In the last column, have them explain their casting decisions. Remind them they cannot cast themselves in any role and that they must try to ignore their friendships within the group. Their goal is to cast the parts to bring forth the best possible production, and they must be able to explain the reason behind their casting decisions.

Once they have "cast" the show, have them turn in the papers to you without including their own names. Assemble the group and go through the sheets, announcing the different choices for the leading roles. Read out the reasoning for the decisions. If time permits, go through the choices for some of the secondary roles.

This exercise may show that everyone has actually chosen the person you were thinking of, anyway. Or it may show widely different choices, which may lead you to take greater care in explaining your own reasoning behind your casting. At the very least, it shows that casting is an art, not a science, and there is never only one cast. However, you must choose one possible cast, and you must present it with confidence and the assurance that it will help the entire group "bring forth the best possible production."

Chapter 8
A Typical Rehearsal

Once you have cast the show, you can begin rehearsals in earnest. Although types of rehearsals and general tips for rehearsal management are given in chapter 3, this section gives more detail on structuring and running a rehearsal.

From the time you have finished the initial walk-through until all scenes are prepared and you are ready to begin complete, nonstop run-throughs, we have found the following structure works well. Assuming a two-hour session once a week, you will spend about half the time on dialog scenes and the other half on singing and dance sequences. This structure, of course, can be modified to suit your particular schedule. Occasionally you may need to focus an entire session on musical numbers in order to make best use of the musical director's availability.

It is very difficult to keep the group interested for a two-hour session that rehearses dialog scenes or musical numbers only. Try to include some singing, dancing, and dialog in each two-hour session. If you are willing to learn the fundamentals of conducting singers and teaching dance routines, you should have no problem rehearsing many of the song and dance numbers yourself.

Activities

Administration (10 minutes)

Assemble the group and explain what will be happening that day. Hand out any props that might be used. Take attendance; collect fees; and, at rehearsals later in the schedule, sell tickets.

Singing warm-up (15–20 minutes)

First, direct the entire group, whether or not they will be in the actual number during the performances, to sing through a couple of the big chorus numbers from the show. Use recorded or live music for accompaniment. If your performers have learned the dance movements in previous sessions, ask them to do the movements as well as sing. Otherwise, they can sit or stand and sing the songs.

Some directors like to use a "pre-singing warm-up," where the singers run through some scales or even musical tongue twisters. For this age group, it is usually just as effective simply to start singing the songs (or the chorus lines from several songs, once the group knows most of the show tunes). However, some singing warm-ups are described in chapter 10.

During the singing warm-up, do not attempt to stop the group and coach any specifics. The purpose of this exercise is to warm up their voices and to get their attention on the musical. Your group will just get frustrated if you constantly stop and correct them. You may say a couple positive things, such as "This sounds very strong today!" or "I liked the way Jeannie threw her hands up in such a big, definite motion there at the end," but keep the momentum, enthusiasm, and fun going for the first couple of songs.

Second, ask the entire group to go through a couple of numbers where they might have — or have already been having — problems. Perhaps they are hitting wrong notes, getting off rhythm, or facing some other challenge, such as often happens in "Who Will Buy?" from *Oliver* or "Luck Be a Lady Tonight" from *Guys and Dolls*, where singers come in at different times.

Again, do not stop the group once they have started singing. At the end of the song, point out the section that they need to correct. Avoid piling up too many negatives or making comments, such as "That was terrible, I don't see how you will ever get this together if you don't try harder," etc., even though you may, occasionally, truly feel that way. Instead, concentrate on telling them as specifically and simply as possible what they need to do to make it better, and have them do it again.

For specific tips on coaching singing, see chapter 10.

Movement and dance sequence rehearsal (35 – 40 minutes)

As a warm-up to this section, run through one of the big cast dance numbers you taught during the audition or another they have already learned. Again, require everyone to participate, even if they are not in the scene.

Start the music and begin working on the dance routine as soon as a few players have assembled themselves on the stage. Don't wait for everyone to get on-stage; you will wait forever. Once a few people start dancing, the rest of the group will get the message and join in.

During the first number, which they supposedly already know and is simply a warm-up, do not stop and coach. Confine your remarks to positive ones. For example: "Good, you all turned the same way," or "Very precise movements!"

Then concentrate on teaching the next big dance number on your plan. Expect everyone to learn the dance even if ultimately, for reasons of plot, they will not appear in the actual scene. No one should be off-stage chatting. You never know when you will need someone to fill in for an absent player.

Concentrate on teaching the basic steps and hand motions. Coach with positive comments and praise the actors who are actually doing it well. For example: "Well remembered — think — what comes next?" or "Nice arms, Kimberly."

For specifics of developing and teaching dance numbers, see the section "Choreography" in chapter 10.

Break (10 minutes)

As the rehearsals progress, the performers — and you — will appreciate the break! Work on dialog scenes commences after the break, so your group can use this time find their scripts, look at the scene, find substitute or the real props, and even review their lines if they are at that stage of the rehearsal schedule.

Dialog scenes (35 minutes)

In rehearsing the dialog scenes, work through the play, starting at the beginning and going through each scene in order. Your group should all be in the audience, each armed with a script and a pencil, each watching the action and getting onto the stage when it is their turn. This way your players will become increasingly familiar with the show's running order.

When you are still using scripts, be sure to "signpost" your players clearly, saying the page number on which you want them to begin. Once a few actors are in place, begin the scene, even if two actors start reading all five parts. If you wait for everyone to assemble, you can use up half the rehearsal time and in the process, become very cross indeed. The missing actors will join the scene. If it turns out the actor is actually absent from the rehearsal, ask a player not in the scene to "read in" that actor's part. Try not to skip rehearsing a scene if actors are missing. It's unfair to the actors who have actually come.

In the course of your rehearsals, you will work through the dialog scenes several times. One session should be a walk-through of the entire play, including song and dance numbers. Then several sessions should be dedicated to blocking the main stage action. Further rehearsals should focus on working the action and polishing the performance in terms of timing, characterization, stage business, projection, and energy. For further details about rehearsing dialog scenes, see chapter 9.

Final dance and movement number (5 minutes)

Before the close of the session, ask the group to assemble to perform a final dance scene, preferably one you have *not* worked on that day. If your group hasn't learned enough numbers to draw on at this point in the rehearsal schedule, get them to stand and sing any large number they haven't worked on that day. In this way, you end the session on a fresh and interesting note.

The close (5 minutes)

Recap what you have done that day and tell them what you will do the following session. Ask them to look through the pages they will be working on the following week. Collect any borrowed scripts, song sheets, props, or costumes, and oversee tidying up.

Questions and Comments from Your Cast

If nothing else, expect a wide range of unsolicited and sometimes puzzling observations, comments, and questions from your group members during the rehearsal process. These might range from "I've learned all my lines" at the second session of rehearsal to "I was sick last week and left my script here two weeks ago. Have you seen it?"

It may seem odd, but you will frequently be asked, "Who am I playing?" Actually, because you will often have actors playing several roles, you too may be asking this question — for example, "Who's playing Benny Southstreet/Harry the Horse/Society Max?"

Chapter 9

Preparing Dialog Scenes

In our rehearsal plan, each two-hour session devotes about thirty to forty minutes to preparing dialog scenes.

Walk-Through (1 Session)

This rehearsal takes place immediately after the show is cast. Unlike most of your rehearsals, it does not follow the "typical rehearsal structure" as outlined in the previous chapter. You will need the entire two-hour session to walk through the action of the musical.

A walk-through rehearsal is just that: the actors walk through the action of the scenes, including songs and dances, holding their scripts and saying their lines. The main goal of the walk-through is for the group to develop a sense of the storyline in its entirety, the order of scenes, and the basic action of each scene. After all, during the auditions, you probably concentrated on a few key scenes and numbers. It may have been several weeks since the group saw the show on video or heard about it in its entirety.

Working with the actors on-stage

Hand out scripts to everyone. These scripts should have any cuts or changes marked in them already so the actors can easily determine when a scene ends or begins. If you are using a rehearsal area on the floor and not the actual stage, make sure your actors know where the audience will be sitting.

Before you begin each scene, spend a couple of minutes asking the group some questions from the following list about the scene they are about to walk through. They can refer to their scripts for the answers. If they have not been on-stage for the previous scene, they have extra time to look in the script before their scene. This exercise helps them to see the script, not always you, as a source of information.

• Where does the scene take place?
• Who is in the scene?
• What happens in the scene?
• What costume is your character wearing?
• What props do you bring on?
• How long after the last scene does this scene take place?

Performers may not be able to answer these questions immediately. Sometimes this information is not stated explicitly in the stage directions but emerges through later dialog and actions. It may seem obvious who is in the scene, but some scripts have the confusing practice of putting the characters' lines next to their last names (MR. BROWN or MISS BLACK) while the actual characters address each other by first names ("My dear Veronica," "My darling Harold"). Encourage the group to figure out as much as they can by themselves, without relying on you.

Don't spend a lot of time digging out the answers or rifling through the script. Avoid divulging the answers yourself. Rather, encourage them to keep reviewing their scripts and watching the show if not on-stage, and see if they can find out for themselves.

Work through the entire script, from start to finish. If you come to a big singing number, ask everyone to get up on-stage and perform it if they have learned the routine during auditions, or just to stand or sit and sing it while you play the music if they have not. For solos and duets, you may want the actors to sing just a few stanzas. When actors finish being on-stage, instruct them to sit in the audience area, watch the other scenes, and get ready to go back on-stage when required.

Once the actors are on-stage, don't try to "block" the action or give any kind of specific action. Other than occasional admonitions to face the audience or not stand directly in front of others for a long time, allow the performers to stand or sit however they wish. Don't specify where exits and entrances are. If you are asked anything, simply say, "I want you to just make it up this time." Don't worry if the locations of entrances and exits change halfway through a scene or between scenes. Don't coach how a line should be said.

The players may want to carry a pencil and make their own notes, but you should not be giving them notes of any kind. You may want to have a pencil yourself, so you can record any interesting movements or line interpretations that might work in the actual performance.

This tactic of not providing any blocking or other direction forces the actors to think for themselves: about what the words mean, toward whom they would be directing certain lines, which character they would be standing near to or far from, where they might be coming from, and so forth. This tactic of not blocking also forces the actors to pay attention to what is going on in the script, and if they are not on-stage, to follow the action of the entire play and see where they come into the action.

Another advantage of not giving blocking or other direction during the walk-through is that you get ideas from the actors as they try things out. For example, a car chase in *Bugsy Malone* once expanded into the audience because the actors themselves chose to do so during the initial walk-through.

Activities for actors not on-stage

Because the walk-through rehearsals progress without interruption and include the song and dance numbers, no one should be sitting around for very long. If someone is sitting around quite a bit, consider why and determine if they could join a chorus number.

From the audience, performers can see what the action of the play is about, as it will happen in *their* show, not the video. It's one thing to watch and follow the action of a professional video. However, your performers must learn the script — which may be quite different from the filmed version — as their particular group will enact it. The walk-through also allows the true pace of the scenes to emerge, so those waiting their turn in the audience become aware of how much or how little time they will have off-stage.

The main responsibility of actors not on-stage is to be ready. Actors not in a scene should sit in the audience area and watch the walk-through, moving onto the stage when required. Make it clear that you will *not* remind actors waiting in the audience when it is their turn to go on. They have a script and are watching the action, so they should be able to figure it out. During the walk-through, lavish praise on actors who manage to go on-stage on cue, as this is one skill they will need their entire acting career.

As time goes on, they will learn that being ready is of paramount importance in achieving a good stage performance: entering on cue and with high energy, having lines memorized, staying in character, bringing on the right props, wearing the right costume, picking up cues, reacting realistically, and leaving on cue are all part of being ready.

For now, the main goal of the actors insofar as being ready is concerned is to get on-stage at the right time, read their lines at the right time — ideally directing them to the right person — and exit at the right time.

Encourage the actors in the audience to work out the answers to the questions you pose about the different scenes and to be ready for their next entrance. If you feel they need anything else to think about, ask them to note if they see anything on-stage that they think the audience would enjoy seeing in the actual performance. This helps you capture any ideas or creativity shown by the cast during the walk-through.

Making constructive comments during the walk-through

During the walk-through, any corrective comments should be focused on the actor being easily seen and heard. Try to limit such comments to no more than one per actor. Keep them short and objective, always referring to the actors by their character names. For example,

"Fat Sam, I can't hear you!"

"Nathan, face the audience!"

"Sarah, speak more loudly!"

"Ghoul, move so I can see Christine!"

You can also make short laudatory comments during the action, taking particular care to compliment those who remember to enter and exit at the right time and are ready:

"Oliver, good entrance!"

"Fagin, good volume!"

"Sarah, perfect timing during your exit!"

"Gus, nice turn!"

Avoid giving direction regarding characterization during the walk-through.

Because you are trying to complete the walk-through in a single two-hour session, you will usually not have time for extended comments, that is, comments made after a scene is finished and the actors are no longer on-stage. Your group may become bogged down in just working out the action.

However, if you do have the time, you can record and make such comments at the end of a scene or act, or at the end of the entire walk-through. If you do make any comments at the end, as always, appeal to your players' interest in being excellent actors. Make comments in the form of "Good actors do X, and such-and-such deserve our praise because they have also done so." For example, you might say, "Good actors enter with energy. We saw Dodger and Charlie do this today," or "Fagin is picking up his cues quickly! This helps maintain pace within the scene." Keep your comments short, positive, and specific, and use the characters' names as much as possible.

Blocking Rehearsals (5 Sessions)

Once you have completed the first walk-through, you are ready to block the action, that is, assign the movements the actors will take on-stage. Each session follows the structure outlined in chapter 8 and includes work on song and dance numbers as well as on blocking the dialog scenes.

Preparing a blocking plan

Blocking refers to deciding where actors will stand on-stage and to where they will move. It is very difficult to create blocking during an actual rehearsal. You need to work out the blocking before the rehearsal, record it on your master script, and know how you will communicate it to your group.

Before you can plan the blocking for the scene, you need to draw out a floor plan for each scene indicating where the furniture and other set pieces are arranged on the stage and the location of any fixed entrances or off-stage focus points. In order for you to tell the actor where to enter from or what point to, you need to know, for example, on which side of the stage Carlotta's dressing room is or in what direction the Salvation Army Mission lies.

Some scripts provide detailed set plans and stage directions that include almost every move by every character. If you have such a script, you simply need to work out the blocking plan from the information provided. No matter how detailed the stage directions may be, we still recommend that you work out a formal blocking plan before the rehearsal and record it in your master script.

Other scripts limit stage directions to little more than "enter" or "exit" and provide no floor plan whatsoever. If you have such a script, you will have to work out your set plan and stage directions in detail for yourself. Draw on the expertise of your set designer if you are fortunate to have someone to help you in this role. Otherwise, read through the entire play and sketch floor plans of each scene on a sheet of paper. Label the floor plan clearly with its location and the act/scene number or numbers. You may end up with a total of several floor plans, some of which may consist of a bare stage with arrows pointing to what is off-stage in either direction.

In planning the initial blocking of the scene, you may wish to use ideas from some of the spontaneous blocking of your walk-through or sketch out ideas on a napkin in a restaurant. However, to finalize them you need to sit down with each scene and its floor plan. Get a set of pennies, old chess pieces, or other small markers to stand for the characters, and write the characters' initials on the pieces with permanent ink. We don't recommend using cut up pieces of paper or card to stand for characters, because they tend to blow around in the slightest breeze. Work through the action, and move the markers around the floor plan, seeing if you can achieve a sensible blocking plan for everyone.

Once you have finalized your blocking plan, record the blocking in your master script.

Recording blocking

You need to record the blocking for the entire show clearly, and each individual actor needs to record his or her character's blocking. True, everyone memorizes the blocking, but at the first rehearsals, and for a lengthy period afterwards, you and your company need a record of where everyone is and where everyone is supposed to go.

In your master script, use abbreviations for the characters, remembering to find some way to distinguish characters with the same initials. For example, ND = Nathan Detroit, NN = Nicely-Nicely, John Jones = JOJ, James Jones = JAJ. Write a key in the front of the script.

In communicating and recording blocking, you and your group should refer to the traditional stage areas and actor positions. Try to teach this terminology in a short session, ideally before or early in your auditions. See chapter 5 for suggestions. In recording blocking, use the common abbreviations for stage areas and actor positions such as FF, FB, 1/4, R, UL, or UR when you record your blocking and ask your actors to do the same.

Relate entrances and exits to the actual stage, if used. For example, curtains on either side have three legs, so clarify from which leg the actor is to make an entrance or exit.

Use arrows and Xs to indicate movement. Other movements may need to be written out fully. Some examples of blocking notation are as follows:

XDL – (Cross Down Left)

XD&R of Oliver – (Cross Down and Right of Oliver)

Hide US of bed – (Hide upstage of bed)

Grab basket

↳ Nathan – (Turn counterclockwise and face Nathan)

↑ plat – (Jump on platform)

You can also record blocking in your master script with thumbnail sketches of stick figures.

If movements are to take place at precise moments in a dialog, you and the actor can indicate this in the script by drawing a line from the written dialog to the blocking notation. See figure 12.

Recording Blocking Precisely in Dialog
(from *Phantom of the Op'ry*, p. 32)

MRS. SWANSONG: We'd better get your things from the teamster's wagon, dear. — *XR*

CHRISTINE: Yes, mother.

FARLEIGH: Allow me to assist, ma'am. — *XL Between ladies*

MRS. SWANSONG: Farleigh? You here? ↳

FARLEIGH: I wrote you I'd be here.

MRS. SWANSONG: That's right, you did. I forgot. — *Sits*

Figure 12 – Example of blocking notation in a script

Creating meaningful blocking

Blocking needs to be meaningful in relation to the lines being spoken, the traits of the characters on-stage, and current developments in the plot. This helps the actors remember their lines and helps the audience understand the story. Blocking also needs to be creative to keep the audience interested. Audiences don't want to see actors standing, in a straight line, center stage, each scene. At the same time, blocking needs to make the actors visible to the audience as much as possible.

Here are some basic tips to help you create meaningful blocking:

- Arrange the actors so they all can be seen as clearly as possible. If the audience can't see the characters, they won't know what is going on.
- Arrange actors to emphasize the importance or status of a particular character. If Nathan Detroit is the leader, giving lots of information to the others, place him at the apex of a triangle, with the other characters spread out along the two sides of the triangle, looking upstage at him.
- Characters move for a reason. They may move out of emotion or to emphasize a point. They may move toward or away from another character out of like or dislike, fear, or contempt. However, avoid pointless zig-zagging around the stage. Movement on every line becomes tedious to watch and distracts from the storyline.
- Aim for variety in vertical levels to provide interest and emphasis. For example, if characters are crowding around another to hear a story, have some of them perched on the platform (if platforms are being used in the scene), some kneeling or sitting, some leaning far forward. In group scenes, ask the actors to try variations — sitting, kneeling, lying down, bending down, stretching up — see how it looks.
- Stage business can lead to interesting blocking. What could a character be doing that is not too distracting but helps show their personality or state of mind and creates interest? Could some of the orphans in *Oliver* be kicking a rag ball around? Or could the orphans in *Annie* be cuddling rag dolls?
- Never be afraid to change something. Simply announce, "I'm changing this."

Running blocking rehearsals
Working with actors on-stage

For each scene, set out any furniture or set pieces using chairs or tables. Explain where the entrances and exits are. It may be possible to use masking tape to help you place the pieces from one rehearsal to the next. However, if you are in a rented venue on a weekly basis, that tape could easily disappear from one week to the next. Setting pieces in approximate places is usually sufficient, and your actors need to stay flexible and not become dependent on taking exactly four steps when they say a particular line.

Actors should have their scripts and a pencil to record the blocking. The actors *must* write down all moves in the script. Otherwise they will forget movements and the group will stand around in awkward clumps the entire scene. You may need to spend a bit of time giving them some practice in recording blocking. They will find it easiest to use the same notation as you do, as described earlier.

As you give out the blocking, try to explain the reasons behind it, with comments such as, "You gangsters move downstage and to the left so I can see those three molls," or "When you say, 'Oh, what's the use?' you are disgusted so you move away from Tom to downstage right, next to Joanna who may give you some sympathy. This also clears a space for Joe. Joe, enter from up left and cross to center stage."

At all times, remind them to write down the blocking: "Sam, did you note that upstage cross I just gave you?" or "Hot box girls, write this down and then make the move."

During the blocking rehearsal, don't get sidetracked into working on characterization, line delivery, or even the detail of movements, except for an occasional passing comment: "Granny would move slowly, as if her bones ached, wouldn't she?"

When you come to a dance scene, if the chorus is not already on-stage, explain where the chorus members are expected to enter from, and then ask them to do so and to carry on and perform the actual number if they have already learned it. If they haven't already learned the routine, they can still sit or stand and sing the song. It is important that they do the whole number. First, they always need the practice. Second, if other characters are on-stage, they need to start thinking about what they are going to do during the number.

Once you have given the blocking for the scene, get the actors to walk through the blocked scene in its entirety. This gives them a chance to see if they can remember the blocking and to check that they have recorded it correctly. If you are short on time during these repetitions of the scene, you run the blocking moves that get the chorus to the right place on-stage for a number, perform just the beginning of the number, and then skip to the end.

Activities for actors not on-stage

In our rehearsals, blocking dialog scenes takes place after an hour of learning and practicing song and dance routines, so most actors not on-stage are perfectly happy to sit back for a while and watch the dialog rehearsal. Also, because you include any song or dance numbers as they occur, these actors probably won't be sitting very long.

However, you can still ask your group to think about the action and their characters as they watch. Here are some possible questions you might ask them:

- What kind of people are the characters you see on the stage? How old are they?
- Would you like to be their friend in real life? How do you feel about them from your character's point of view?
- How should different characters move or stand? Quickly, slowly, gracefully, clumsily?

As chorus members, the actors are portraying characters who may have strong feelings toward the lead characters. The orphans in *Annie* and *Oliver* obviously react in strong ways to Miss Hannigan and Mr. Bumble; the characters in *Phantom of the Op'ry* have strong feelings toward the Phantom. By thinking about these questions, the chorus members have an opportunity to think about the emotions of their own characters and how to portray them when they do appear on-stage.

The players not on-stage can also give those on-stage some feedback on how well they are communicating with the audience. In any rehearsal, you can always ask those in the audience to make recommendations about the following:

- What, if anything, are the actors doing that is good from the audience's point of view?

107

• What, if anything, would you want to change about what the actors are doing that would help the audience understand the scene better or enjoy it more?

If time permits at the end of each scene, ask those who have been in the audience to give their opinions. Alternatively, have them capture their points on lists headed "what works" and "what needs to be changed."

Working the Action (12 Sessions)

These rehearsals, which total about twelve two-hour sessions, use the same singing-dancing-dialog structure as the walk-through and blocking rehearsals. In these rehearsals, you go through each scene, working through every detail of blocking, characterization, body language, projection, stage business, and the use of properties.

A major goal of these rehearsals is to help your actors create and sustain interesting characters whose actions can be easily seen, whose motivations and moods are easily understood, and whose voices can be easily heard. During the introduction to the show and audition sessions, you have spent time explaining the broad character traits of the different roles. In the walk-through and blocking rehearsals, you introduce the main movements and groupings of the characters. In this set of rehearsals, you focus on refining movements and building unique character traits.

In coaching the movements, body language, and voices of your performers, you will be trying to strike a delicate balance between being realistic enough to be believable, and being large enough to be seen and heard in the back row. Part of this balance will come from the style of the script itself — a melodramatic spoof will call for broader, more exaggerated action and gestures than a romantic comedy. As a director, you must decide which way to push the presentation.

Working a scene — basic structure

The actors will still have their scripts at this point, although you may, toward the end of the set of sessions, start asking them to learn lines of some scenes. Ask them each to have a pencil on-stage so they can make notes. As usual, keep a supply on hand to lend out if necessary.

For each dialog scene you work, first run through the scene, reminding the actors of any basic blocking, such as where they enter from the "front door," or exit to the "kitchen." Prompt them to refer to the blocking notes that they should have recorded in their scripts. If necessary, wait for them to write the blocking down in their scripts. Then go through the scene again slowly, concentrating on a page, or even half-page, at a time.

As the actors go through each page, stop the action whenever you want to give direction or discuss what is happening on-stage. Alternatively, simply shout a brief instruction, such as "Nora should be quite upset during these lines" in hopes that the actress will respond by becoming more upset. In some instances, for example, if some of your players keep their backs turned, it may more be effective to maneuver the actors around the stage physically. Then stop the action and ask them, "Why did I do that?" If you give any direction that you particularly want them to remember, remind them to make notes in their scripts: "Minerva, bang your fist on the dressing table when you say that line."

Many more ideas of what to look for and what kinds of directions to give your actors as you work the action are given in the rest of this section. Try out different approaches with your group and see what is most effective and fun.

After you have done a stop-start version of the page or half-page, run through the entire page without stopping. Then run through the next page, stopping and starting. Then run through that page. Then run through pages 1 and 2 together. Then go on to page 3, and so forth. The effect is cumulative, and the actors need the repetition — it may be weeks before they do this scene again.

If the scene has any special physical action, such as a fighting, pouring and serving drinks, elaborate and complex entrances, group scenes with a lot of movement and emotion, now is the time to work everything out so it runs smoothly. Don't expect things to fall into place at the last minute.

As you watch the actors, keep asking yourself: How well do they succeed in getting across the moods, character traits, and intentions of their characters at this particular moment of the musical? If an actress is supposed to be an old lady who has just seen a frightening apparition, does she seem old? Frightened? Does she get this across to the audience clearly? If the character is a young girl who has just been told she has a terrible disease, does she seem shocked? During these rehearsals, you need to try to unlock what works and what doesn't and try to get the actors to keep what works and change what doesn't.

If the actors are not being effective in getting across the storyline or their characters, first try to encourage them to think about their character in greater depth so *they* come up with a better way themselves. Many ideas are given in the remainder of this section to help your performers foster their own creativity.

However, this hands-off approach doesn't work with everyone. Don't be shy about simply assigning actions to the actors to help them communicate the mood of the scene or the emotions of the characters. Give them specific things to try: "Sam, slump in the chair on that line — because you are very upset" or "Christina, stamp your foot when George says that — because you are so angry you can't even speak" or "Put your hands on your hips on that line and glare at Sandra. You have just had enough." Remember, your performers may be inexperienced, may not have much confidence in themselves, and just want to get on with the show.

Helping the actors to understand the dialog

Take time to discuss the dialog and make sure the actors understand all the vocabulary and expressions their characters use. As you work through each page, ask questions to test their understanding of the words on the page. For example, you might ask, "What does 'all made up' mean?" "How does the cleaning woman feel about rats if another character says she 'can't abide' them?" or "What do the words 'decreed' and 'decreeing' mean?" If the actors don't understand what the lines mean, they can hardly be expected to declaim them with the correct expression.

You may need to explain the references and allusions used in some plays, as they can be outside the experience of your young performers — prohibition, workhouse, swansong, opera/op'ry, for instance.

It is also helpful to make sure they understand any words used in parentheses by the author to describe the character or the way the character delivers a line. Words like "agitated" or "flummoxed" or "depressed" may be unfamiliar to many children.

Questions that can help actors to develop effective characterization

Before you begin to work a page or half-page, you may ask the actors questions so they will think about character motivation and development. You may not necessarily do this for each page, but such questions can help the actors focus on the motivations, moods, and traits of the characters they portray. These questions might include the following:

- Why are you here? If you are entering the stage at the start of the scene, where did you just come from?
- What mood are you in? Why?
- What plans or intentions do you have? What are you thinking about?
- If you now see another character, how do you react? Why? Were you expecting to see them? Do you already know something about them that influences your feelings and reactions?
- Is there any stage business your character might be doing during this part of the scene?

Remind them that their job as actors is to communicate these moods, characteristics, intentions, and reactions clearly to the audience. As they act out the scene, actors need to get across to the audience whatever state the character is in. What state are they in at the beginning? Perhaps they are supposed to enter in a jolly mood, having just won the football game. Or they are discovered on-stage in a dejected mood because their teacher has just assigned ten pages of homework. As the scene progresses, does the character's mood change? Why? What other emotion does the character's mood change into? How can this emotion be shown to the audience?

Using props

In working the action rehearsals, the actors should start using real or substitute props. Encourage the actors to tell *you* what props they will need in the following scene. This helps the off-stage actors in the audience to stay alert because they need to be thinking about what they might be bringing on-stage with them and finding something — in some cases, anything — to take on-stage when their turn comes.

To help the actors start to take responsibility for their props, be prepared to ask questions such as the following during the action on the stage:

- Where is your mop?
- What action should you be doing with that line? Might it not be helpful if you had the hairbrush/magazine/gun?
- What is Miss Hannigan's gin bottle doing in the middle of Daddy Warbucks' office?

During this set of rehearsals, start discussing scene changes with the cast: What items and scenery will be needed in each scene? Who will be responsible for bringing things on or taking things off? It may take some time to see who is available and who is actually able to help with changes, because helping with scene changes takes focus and concentration. See the section, "Planning and Rehearsing Scene Changes" in chapter 14.

Changing the scene sequence

During these sessions, depending on the script, you may want to work through the scenes in an order different from that in the script. The first time, work your way through the scenes as they occur in the play, one after another. This reminds the actors of the correct plot sequence and helps them think about changing their costumes, picking up props, etc. The second time, if possible, work your way through the scenes in order that the characters would play them. This helps the players capture the mood of their characters from scene to scene. For example, in *Guys and Dolls*, go through all the scenes with Adelaide and then all the scenes with Sarah. They don't actually meet each other, or know much about each other, until the end of the play.

Tools of communicating character and action

In getting across the moods and traits of their characters, your actors have four major tools of communication. As you watch the action, see if you can make any suggestions — or help the actor come to his or her own realization — of a character's posture, body language, movements, speech, and facial expressions.

Body language and posture

Is the character's posture and stance tense, straight, slumped? Are gestures economical and terse or large and extravagant? Does the character move quickly or slowly? Awkwardly or gracefully? In addition to expressing mood and character, the actors need to keep their bodies turned to the audience as much as possible so they can be seen.

Facial expression

Does the expression on the character's face match his or her mood? Or is the character trying to hide something? Actors also need to keep their faces turned toward the audience as much as possible so their expressions can be seen.

Vocal intonation

Does the vocal inflection match the character's mood and age? If the character were heard only, and not seen, would the audience still know who it was? Is there variety in pitch and volume? The actors must also enunciate words clearly and project their voices so they can be easily heard.

Movements in relationship to other characters on the stage

Do two characters stand or sit near each other? Far from each other? Does one turn away from the other? Is one on a higher or lower plane, towering over or crouching down, or on a higher or lower platform? If you have previously told George to sit on the couch next to Sally, he may want to refine this movement so he sits even closer to (or farther from) Sally, with his head turned toward her or away from her, depending on their moods and relationship. In addition to this, actors need to stay visible to the audience and not block others or allow themselves to be blocked from view.

Making constructive comments during working the action rehearsals

In these rehearsals, your performers should strive to refine their use of these communication tools. In discussing your actors' performances, it is helpful to refer to them. It makes your comments, especially ones of direction or correction, seem less personal and negative. It also makes your positive comments less subjective.

If your actors are being effective in getting the storyline and their characters across, tell them so, so they will do it again next time. As the action unfolds on-stage, you can make comments such as, "Nathan, keep that gesture, works great," or "Ghoul, your intonation was scary and perfect, keep it!" Insist that they make a note in their scripts of any creative stage business or especially excellent expression so that they will remember it for the next rehearsal.

Activities for actors not on-stage

In these rehearsals, you will go through the dialog scenes page by page, frequently repeating short sections of scenes that need work. You may wish to cut any dance numbers that occur and work only on the dialog. Therefore, you need to pay extra attention to those actors who are *not* on-stage. If you follow our rehearsal structure, you can concentrate on the on-stage actors with minimum disruption from those off-stage.

Because you have spent the first hour rehearsing the dance numbers, many group members will happily sit back and watch the action for forty minutes as they await their own entrances. They need to stay attentive; although they may not have a song for a couple of scenes, chorus members are often still involved in the action and will need to be on-stage at some point — for example, when Bill Sykes gets shot in *Oliver*.

To keep them interested in watching what is happening on-stage, ask them to watch the stage action and "play director" (see following section). Set questions for them to answer about the action. You may get some good ideas for the show this way, and it will help your actors, who may be inexperienced and have only a chorus role, learn some of the challenges of larger, more demanding roles.

That aside, you will probably want to schedule a few extra rehearsals for scenes with only a few actors, especially if they are romantic in nature or if a particular scene is floundering and you need to have a heart-to-heart discussion of why it isn't working.

Playing director

Give those actors in the audience watching the scenes the task of answering some questions for each scene you work through. You may even want to ask certain groups to watch particular characters. If you ask the obvious question: "What was good about this scene?" you will find that kids — like adults — can have a hard time describing the positive, specific points of a scene. They often dive right in with an avalanche of negative comments. Provide them with some ideas of what to look for and some specific examples of what they could say:

- Projecting one's voice — "Bugsy was nice and loud when he said his lines."
- Good vocal expression — "Oliver sounded really sad; I really believed him."
- Good variety in volume — "Warbucks didn't just yell during his speech, he used different tones."
- A good facial expression — "Sky looked really shocked when Nathan pointed to Sarah."
- A good gesture or movement — "Minerva came across as really friendly when she put her arm around Miss Pampermouse's shoulder."
- Creating appropriate stage business — "Nicely-Nicely shuffling the cards — it was interesting but didn't take away from what the others were saying."
- Good timing, particularly during a comic scene.
- Stayed in character even when not talking — "The two pink ladies were good — the way they concentrated on listening to what Rizzo was saying."

In addition to looking for good things about the scene, you also want them to make suggestions about what could be improved. So your second question is, "What one thing would you suggest to make the scene even better or even more interesting to the audience?"

Again kids, like adults, need practice in phrasing advice in positive, not negative terms, so provide some examples:

- "Adelaide needs to speak up when she says 'Nathan, I wrote my mother we were married,' not "Adelaide was so quiet no one can possibly hear her."
- "Noah needs to be scarier to Oliver. Perhaps he could lean over Oliver when he talks to him," not "Noah couldn't scare a fly."

Other activities

Off-stage actors can also be encouraged to do the following:

- Look at their own lines and practice the lyrics of the songs
- Think about what props they will need for the next scene
- Think about what costume they need to change into for the next scene

• Create some stage business for their character to try out in the next scene — for example, tying a shoe, filing nails, brushing hair, arm-wrestling, or wringing out a dishcloth.

Building Your Actors' Technical Skills

During the course of your rehearsals, you may come to realize that your players, either individually or as a group, may need to develop some of the more technical skills of acting — for example, projecting their voices, enunciating words, and learning lines. If you are working in a hall of any size larger than a typical classroom or living room, your actors need to know how to project their voices, and you need to help them. Lines need to be memorized, and you can give them tips on how to approach this task.

Improving volume and enunciation

Although your actors may develop excellent and interesting characters, some may need to increase their volume of speech and enunciate their words more precisely. We find that although microphones are helpful during solo or duet *songs*, amplifying spoken voices during dialog scenes is unnecessary and runs counter to the spirit of theatrical performance.

Here are some tips to use when working to improve your actors' projection:

• Projecting your voice is not the same as shouting. You should not strain your vocal cords or hurt your throat when you talk on-stage.

• Neither can you simply speak normally. Not only do the other characters (who may be only be a few feet away and whom you are facing), need to hear you, but the entire audience (who may be fifty to one hundred feet away), also needs to hear and understand every word.

• When you speak, think of pushing the sound out, toward the back of the audience. Push your voice through your nasal cavities and over those membranes, not just through your mouth. Doing this will *not* make you sound like you have a bad cold; it will make your voice richer and fuller and easier to hear. Nasal membranes act like a drum or strings on a piano or guitar. They act to reverberate and amplify sound.

Here are some exercises and games to use with the group to help raise their volume levels:

• Perform a few lines of the play, not necessarily from a scene they are in. First, shout the scene. Then repeat the scene in normal voices. Then repeat the scene in a good theatrical voice. Sometimes performing the contrasts helps the actors find the right level of volume.

• Come to the front of the stage. Say the lines toward the audience, trying to reverberate the sounds off the wall, creating an echo effect. Now try the lines as if you were acting them, again trying to create an echo effect.

• Perform a few lines of the play as if someone were watching with a telescope from some distance away. Raise the voice level so the onlooker can hear as well as see "up close."

• Pair those with weak projection skills with stronger performers. Ask them to take turns in matching each other's vocal levels for two consecutive but identical dialog scenes. Ask the audience which scene they could understand the best and why.

• Practice stage whispers. This exercise helps underline the importance of speaking clearly and demonstrates to the group another way of using the voice on-stage.

Another challenge for many young performers is enunciation, or how clearly words are pronounced. The challenge is doubled if they are attempting an accent. It is particularly helpful if you can give the actors an example of any particular words they have trouble with, along with the correct enunciation. Here are some tips to help improve enunciation:

• Try to hit the consonants clearly and precisely. This will help with both enunciation and projection.

• Make sure the vowels resonate. Don't swallow your words.

• Slow down. Actors who speak too quickly cannot be understood. Pause between thoughts.

Depending on the age group, you may need to explain what consonants and vowels are. Some ideas for exercises and games to help improve enunciation are:

• Before rehearsing dialog scenes, try some tongue twisters.

• Ask the actors to act out a short scene from the play. In the first version, they should make the enunciation as sloppy as possible. In the second, make it over-enunciated.

117

• Pair actors who have good enunciation with some who do not. Ask them to act out a short scene twice, each time matching the other in clarity of speech. Ask the audience to comment on which version was easiest to understand and why.

Learning lines and performing memorized scenes

By the time your show has reached the last third of the rehearsal schedule — the "polishing" rehearsals — the performers should know their lines. Therefore, you need to help them learn their lines during the time you are working the action.

One approach is to ask the actors to learn the lines of a scene they just worked on for the following sessions. For example, if you have worked on act 2, scene 3 today, ask them to learn the lines act 2, scene 3 for next week. At the next rehearsal, after the warm-ups, ask the question, "Who's learned their lines?" Lavish praise on those who say they have, and run through the scene without scripts on-stage. If someone is missing, have another actor read in that character's lines. Don't let the other actors off the hook from their own responsibilities of learning lines.

Once the scene is over, again praise those who did indeed learn their lines and those who seemed to have tried to. If someone had to use the script, now is the time to make brief comments such as, "I couldn't see the expression on the doctor's face because her nose was in her script!" or "I couldn't hear Sky Masterson because he kept looking down at the script." These comments reinforce the value of the actor's performances but remind them that they do themselves no favors by not learning their lines.

Using a prompt

Whenever you have no scripts on-stage, you need someone to fill the role of the prompt. The prompt is responsible for helping actors who have forgotten their lines to get going again. You should not fill this role yourself — as director, you need to be looking at the stage action at all times, not the script. During dress rehearsals and performances, the prompt needs to be an adult assigned specifically to the role, sitting just off-stage or in the front row of the audience. During the initial scenes performed with "no books," any off-stage actor can be recruited to be the prompt and can sit with you in the audience. As the rehearsals progress, a couple of kids will probably become your unofficial prompts when they are not on-stage themselves.

Some directors are totally against the idea of using a prompt, but we have found that young performers have more confidence if they have the security of a prompt.

The prompt needs a special "prompt script" marked up to show any changes to lines or action, as well as pauses before a line begins or continues.

The prompt needs certain skills to execute the job properly. He or she needs to watch the action, not just the script, and judge when prompting is necessary. For example, if the character first has to search silently through a cabinet and then say, "I can't find the jewels," the prompt should wait until the stage business is completed before deciding the actor has forgotten her lines. Also, if someone forgets to enter on time, it is especially hilarious when the prompt says the line of someone not actually on-stage! The prompt should just give a few words of the line, not the entire line, in hopes that the actor will carry on from there. For example, in the situation above, the prompt should say, "I can't find" instead of, "I can't find the jewels! What fiend could have taken them?" On the other hand, it is vital to give enough of the line. It would be no use giving, "I." Give significant words. In Annie, it would be no use giving a propt, "Annie." How many characters say her name in that show?

Tips for learning lines

Learning lines is not a natural skill. If your group members attend schools where they are asked to memorize poetry or other passages, you are in luck. More likely, you will need to teach them this skill yourself. Here are some pointers for them.

Preparing to learn lines:

- Don't try to learn everything in one sitting at the last minute. Concentrate on learning the lines the director asks you to, by the date the director asks you to — for example, act 2 scene 3 for next week.

- Remember you need to learn *what* you say (lines) and *when* you say them (cues). Especially when you are working on a scene that has many short lines by different characters in rapid succession, it's easier if you memorize your entire cue line as well as your own line.

- You may feel more comfortable if you work alone as you learn your lines, because it involves saying your lines out loud. Once you know your lines, ask someone to read in the other parts so you don't have access to the script and cannot peek.

- Make it your goal to memorize each line exactly as written. Remember, other actors will be awaiting their cues from you and are greatly helped if you say them precisely as written. So take the trouble to learn "He ran fast," not "He went fast."
- If you are learning a scene of several pages, concentrate on learning a half-page at a time. Then put two half-pages together, then a page and a half, then two pages, and so forth.
- If you are learning a series of short lines, take one line with its cue at a time. If one of your "lines" actually has several sentences, take it a sentence at a time. Learn one sentence or cue and line completely. Then learn the next. Then recite both together. Then learn a third cue and line or sentence. Then take the three of them together, and so on, until you have learned a half-page. Then work on the next half-page in the same way. Then put two half-pages together. Then one and one-half page. And so forth.
- If you have a very long speech — say of ten sentences or more — see the section on "Learning long speeches" below.

Learning lines and cues:

- Sit with the script and a blank piece of paper. Read the cue *and* your actual line *out loud* several times. Don't read the script silently; you will remember your lines and cues much more easily if you read them aloud. Now cover the line with the paper, look off into space, imagine the scene, and say the cue and the line aloud. Do not worry about expression at this point, unless it helps you to remember the line better.
- Check the script. Did you say the line as written? If you didn't get through the cue/line sequence at all or said it incorrectly, sneak a peek at the script and try again.
- Now try the next line or sentence. Now try both together.
- Go on to line 3. Now try lines 1, 2, and 3 together.
- Carry on until you can say the lines and cues without looking at the script.

Learning long speeches:

- In some ways learning a long speech is easier than learning a series of lines because you only have to learn one cue. However, you must keep the "story" of the speech in mind so you don't blank out on what comes next.

- Break the speech into groups of five or six sentences. Learn the first group of sentences as a whole. Then work on the second group of sentences. Then put both groups together, and so forth.
- Use the same approach as with learning shorter lines. Read the first sentence aloud, then cover the sentence, and finally try saying it without looking at the script. Then try the second sentence, then sentences 1 and 2 together, and so on.
- Because you have no one to provide cues for your next sentence during the speech, you need to have a good, clear understanding of the sequence of ideas (what happens first, second, third) in the speech. Take a piece of paper and draw stick pictures that illustrate the sequence of ideas in the speech. For example, if the speech is about your grandmother and how she used to walk to school in the snow and help with the spring planting, draw a picture of a grandmother, then one of snow, and then one of seeds or small plants. These pictures will help you remember the content of the speech and what comes when.

Practicing lines and cues:

- Having a script nearby, even when it is covered, is quite different from saying the line in response to someone else speaking the cue. To help you learn your cues and practice your lines, it worthwhile to tape-record the other lines in the scene. Read the other lines of each scene you are in into a tape recorder. Mouth the words of your own lines *slowly*, pausing for any stage business that may take place before your line begins. When you have recorded the whole show, you can practice your lines by playing back the tape and filling in the silence with your own lines.
- Finally, ask a friend or parent to read the other parts of the scene while you say your lines. They may try to coach you on how to say the line. It is usually best to ignore any advice. Explain you are concentrating on content, not expression. However, if you are uncertain of any of the meanings of the words or references, it can be worth asking your parents about them.

Polishing the Action (12 Sessions)

For the next set of sessions, you need to concentrate on making whole scenes, whole acts, and the whole show fit together, flow smoothly, make sense, and interest the audience. Start building the performance energy, which comes from the actors putting down their scripts, picking up their cues, listening to each other, and reacting realistically.

In contrast to the "working the action" rehearsals, where you continually stopped the action and gave immediate direction, in these rehearsals, you run sections, scenes, and acts without stopping, giving any notes after you complete a run-through.

In these rehearsals, encourage your performers to remember how to do things by themselves without any prompting from you. All the blocking, actions, reactions, emotions, and stage business that were carefully created during the working rehearsals now need to become second nature, yet seem spontaneous to the audience. You will often be saying things such as, "Last time we talked about how the gangsters need to rush in, guns drawn, and frantically search for their enemies. Let's see if we can create that again this time."

One goal of the polishing rehearsals is to help establish the running order of the show in the actors' minds. Because, in many situations, you rehearse over many weeks and break down the play into small sections, the actors often have little sense of how the action of the show fits together, and of the time each scene actually takes.

From a technical point of view, actors need to understand this because they will often have to change costumes quickly, move to the other side of the stage for an entrance, or help out with scene changes. From an acting point of view, each performer needs to understand how their character develops in the playing time of the show. For example, they may have ended one scene in a happy mood, and begin the next scene five minutes later feeling sad. They need to be aware of how quickly their mood has to change, why it has changed, and then communicate the change in mood to the audience. They need to remember exactly what to do on-stage and in what order — during a performance, you can't stop the actors and remind them where to enter from, what props to bring on, or what facial expression to use.

Working with actors on-stage

The actors should start performing without scripts on-stage at this point. Some of your leading actors may struggle with this if they have a lot of lines, but keep hounding them. By the final six rehearsals, absolutely no books should be allowed on-stage.

You will be using a prompt at this point, so the actors will just have to cope as best they can if they haven't learned their lines completely and perfectly. Position the prompt in the audience area or just off-stage. For the first part of the polishing rehearsals, you can simply use whatever off-stage actor is available at the time — you may need two or three prompts per rehearsal. Usually the kids enjoy helping in this role, although they must do it with some skill.

Once performers get rid of their scripts, the actors will suddenly discover they have arms and hands they need to do something with. Keep an eye out for anyone who seems to be particularly awkward with using gestures. At the same time, without their scripts, the actors can finally start to *act*. They can use props freely, they can look each other in the eyes — and try not to giggle — they can put the right volume, pace, and expression into speeches.

The actors should be using props for all rehearsals now. If a prop is particularly valuable, you may want to use a substitute rehearsal prop, but the actors must become accustomed to handling real objects — and keeping track of them, if necessary, between scenes.

During the first polishing rehearsals, you will rehearse a section or scene at a time without stopping. By the final polishing rehearsals, you will run entire acts and then the whole play without stopping.

Along with gaining a sense of continuity, the actors need to concentrate on picking up cues from each other so the pace of the show stays fast and energetic no matter how lugubrious the plot may be at that point. Remind your actors that they need to take a breath a few words before the other actor gives the end of the cue. They can *say* the line slowly, but they must *begin* the line immediately on cue, whether the cue is verbal or visual.

Sometimes a "speed rehearsal" will help actors find pace and energy. A speed rehearsal works best towards the end of the rehearsal schedule, when the actors know all their lines, and you are running entire acts or even the whole show. See the section, "Types of Rehearsals," in chapter 3.

Even as actors gain familiarity with the play, they need to maintain the "illusion of the first time" for the audience. Although they have heard and reacted to certain news ten times in a row, the audience has to believe this is the first time this has ever happened. So, if someone is about to come on-stage, or the phone is about to ring, the actors should definitely *not* look off-stage or at the phone!

Actors need to bring energy onto the stage when they enter. Instruct them to feel confident and "big" when they enter and to speak loudly and confidently. Remind them that everyone who comes on-stage needs to help charge up the "performance battery" of the show. To help them grasp this, demonstrate someone coming into a scene *without* energy and then someone coming into a scene *with* energy. Ask the group which performance they think the audience will enjoy most. Ask them which entrance the other actors will benefit from the most. Point out some of your actors who are successful in doing this and ask them to repeat their entrance.

Each time the actors go through a scene, they must remain in character. Some of them will find this difficult if they are not speaking at the time. Chorus members in particular may find this a challenge if they have to watch and react while the leading character has a long speech or song. Ask them to concentrate on looking at and listening to the other characters, imagining they have never, ever heard these words before and need to understand them for a quiz contest the next day for a huge prize.

Actors need to remember all the gestures and movements they have developed in the working rehearsals. Before you run a scene, help them to do this, by saying, "Remember what we learned when we last worked on this scene, the orphans made all their movements very precisely, and Oliver came in very quickly from stage left to the middle of the stage." At times, you may have to remind some actors of movements, such as "Sam, bang your fist on the table when you say that line so everyone knows you are angry."

While the actors are performing on-stage, make notes about what is good and what needs to be improved. Try to find at least one specific good thing about everyone, especially about someone who tends to lack concentration most of the time. After you have finished running through the scene, section, or act, ask the actors to come out and sit on the apron of the stage or other area and then give them your notes. If something has been very poorly executed, perhaps actors facing upstage when speaking or executing a clumsy fight, have the actors quickly redo the action or lines. Don't go overboard on the directions; each actor will at most only be able to take in one or two suggestions. As when people listen to directions to an address, your actors will tune out after the first couple of instructions.

Your notes and comments at the end of each section you run might include the following:

- "The doctor knows his lines! This really allows him to be in character."
- "Nancy didn't have her basket today — did she leave it in the market?"
- "Did you notice how Sam always turned downstage, not upstage when he turned around? That really helps the audience see the expression on his face."
- "Madame Barracuda projected her voice nice and loudly when she was on-stage. Well done."
- "I could have driven a truck through some of the gaps between the end of one line and the beginning of the next. The doctor said 'I don't know where he is,' and what seemed about ten minutes later the nurse said, 'I do!' Can you two just try those lines in quick succession right now?"
- "Good actors are ready for their cues, and pupils 1, 2 and 3 were brilliant at this today."
- "Good stage discipline means you try to develop your character as much as possible in every rehearsal. The orphans July and Tessie really came across as being cold and shivery in their scene today, and they hung onto Annie's every word."
- "When the policeman came on-stage today, he really seemed to take command of the group. A great entrance!"

Once you have run the scene once and given your notes, go back and run through it again. Then move on to the next scene or group of scenes you wish to rehearse.

Activities for actors not on-stage

If you have cast most actors in as many chorus parts as possible, you should, in most instances, have very few actors not performing.

Actors not on-stage should stay in the audience area and not stray backstage during the polishing rehearsals. Actors you have identified as the core stage crew may become involved in scene changes about halfway through the polishing sessions. See the section, "Preparing and Rehearsing Scene Changes" in chapter 14.

During most polishing rehearsals, at least one actor at any one time will need to be recruited as a prompt, so that is another role an off-stage actor can take.

Ask any actors still in the audience these questions while they are sitting watching scenes:

- "Do you know your lines? If not, get your script, get a partner and work on your lines."
- "What is the next scene you will be in? What character will you play in the next scene? What will be their mood at the beginning of the scene? What costume will you be wearing?"
- "Where does the next scene take place? What needs to be on-stage at the beginning that is different from the scene going on now? What props will you need?" This will help any potential stage crew members start to plan for scene changes.
- "How can you make your part interesting? What will you do to show you are interested in what others are saying and doing?"

You can also ask your group to think about things that might possibly go wrong and how their character would react. They can even work together and come up with a short improvised scene. Here are some examples of situations we have seen happen on-stage:

- The phone keeps ringing after the character picks it up.
- The phone doesn't ring when it is supposed to.
- Another character freezes entirely despite prompting from off-stage.
- Another character forgets his or her entrance.

We have seen this last situation happen during performance a few times and it's always fascinating, if heart-stopping, to see how the performers handle it. Once, the characters on-stage started saying, "Benny! Where is he? We expected him by now. Benny! Where are you?" In another situation where someone didn't enter, the actor carried on the conversation with someone off-stage, "So

126

you think I'm a coward? I'll tell you I'm not! You say I won't take on Bugsy? I say I will!" and so forth.

Oscar presentations

The polishing rehearsals are a good time to start "Oscar presentations" to one member of the cast at each rehearsal, and then at the performances. The performer may get the Oscar for any number of reasons that fit with your main goals and concerns at the time:

- Learning all the lines (finally!).
- Being nice and loud on-stage (when previously the performer has been very quiet).
- Made great entrances, with a high energy level that helped other characters energize.
- Staying attentive and in character even if the role is a small one, reacting realistically.
- Not over-reacting and "mugging."
- Creating an interesting bit of stage business.
- Finally getting a dance routine exactly right.

Try to find some sort of statuette to present, which the actor gets to keep until the next performer wins it. A nice gesture is to have some certificates you can fill out and present to the actor to keep. It works best to present the Oscar at the beginning of one rehearsal for work accomplished during the previous one. The actor can then flourish the statuette all during the session, but you can regain it for safekeeping until the following session.

These Oscars help promote a sense of healthy competition to do well and help your group understand what is important to achieve in a rehearsal. They give you a chance to reward some hardworking chorus members who won't be center stage the nights of the show. If you start presenting Oscars during session 30 and present them during the performances as well, you will be able to recognize about ten cast members.

If you want to try to recognize more than one person each rehearsal, you can announce any runner-up "nominations," Oscar-show style, before making the presentation to the actual winner. This will widen the number of performers that you formally recognize, and you will be surprised how much young actors prize simply being complimented in public and in the presence of their peers.

Chapter 10

Preparing Song and Dance Numbers

Singing

The role of the musical director

This role is crucial to your show's success. Even if you intend to do a production using an accompaniment track during the performance, someone still needs to guide the actors through learning the songs, hitting the right notes, and expressing the mood and content. Someone needs to conduct the singers during the show, when they must come in at the correct time and then keep pace with the accompaniment music. If you intend to use live music, the singers still need help in learning the songs, and *both* singers and accompanists need someone to conduct them during the final rehearsals and performances.

Almost invariably, only a trained musician who can sight-read a score and conduct singers and accompanists can do this role competently. If you personally lack the musical training needed to understand a score, sight-read music, and conduct singers, we would recommend you find someone who can and ask them to be your musical director. This individual may be willing to act as accompanist as well as musical director. In the meantime, you can undertake training to fulfill this role in the future.

This book provides a number of tips on conducting singing so you will be able to move your group forward through several songs per session on your own, assuming you have the accompaniment track of the show's music on hand. On those days that you use live music accompaniment, your musical director can conduct the singers from the piano (assuming he or she is also the accompanist), or you can guide them on your own.

Through careful scheduling and using the skills covered in this book, you will find that you will need the musical director for only a few of the total rehearsals. This will reduce your costs if you are paying him or her a fee, and increase goodwill if he or she is working gratis as a volunteer or as part of his or her role as school music teacher or band director.

Working with singers

Whether or not you have a separate musical director for your show, use live music or an accompaniment track, you will still need to be involved in preparing the players to perform songs during the show. In our experience, both rehearsal management and performances are improved by including song and dance numbers, the bigger the better, in each rehearsal session rather than continually separating dialog scenes from musical numbers. Having your musical director on hand, ready to direct every scene, is impractical.

This section helps you prepare your performers to sing and provides tips on coaching singing, even if you are not particularly musical yourself.

Many of the things you need to remind your singers of are the same things you remind your actors about: breathing, pacing, enunciation. Other issues are more musical, but also straightforward: holding a note or cutting it short, singing in key, and keeping up with the rhythm.

Singing warm-ups at rehearsal sessions

We recommend that you begin each session, including the auditions, with a singing warm-up that consists of one or more songs from the show. By singing show numbers, the cast can start concentrating on the show instead of whatever may have been on their minds before the rehearsal, and they get a chance to practice some of the songs.

If you are using recorded music during the warm-ups, or even while they are learning a song, turn down the volume occasionally so they start to increase their own. You can then bring the volume back up after assessing if they are keeping pace and coming in at the right place. This is a very valuable technique if you will be using an accompaniment track during the performance itself.

129

You may wish to conduct short vocal warm-ups before the group starts singing. Here are some possible ideas:
- Sing a tongue twister such as "red leather, yellow leather," or (in the U.K.) "red lorry, yellow lorry." For each one, go one note lower or higher from where you started. Or sing a longer one, such as "She sells sea shells on the sea shore," going up or down the scales.
- Sing a nursery rhyme in a round. "London's Burning," "Row, Row, Row Your Boat," or even the "Alphabet Song" are possible choices.
- Sing the first line of "Over the Rainbow" from the *Wizard of Oz*. This line is a perfect octave leap. Keep repeating the line, starting a tone higher each time.

Teaching songs — the basics

The group needs to learn the songs first, and then add any movement. It is far too difficult to do both at once. We recommend you first teach the song itself, and then teach the dance routine in the second half of the same session or at the following rehearsal.

In preparing to teach your group a song, review the song and see how it is organized into different stanzas and (usually) a refrain or chorus. See if the song can be divided up in some way. For example, if there are eight different stanzas and a chorus, label the stanzas one to eight, and call the chorus stanza the "chorus" or "refrain." Your goal is to take the group through the song stanza by stanza, building until they can sing the entire song, in tune and with expression, without the song sheet or script.

Typical steps in teaching a song

Cue up the vocal track or have the accompanist ready to play. Direct the group to sing the entire song all the way through without stopping.

After they have sung it through, teach the chorus stanza, if there is one; it must come in vigorously each time it is sung. Then teach the other stanzas. You may want them not to sing the chorus while they are working on the individual stanzas. Then put the chorus and individual stanzas together.

For each stanza you teach, ask the group to chant it first, looking at the song sheet to begin with, then with the song sheet turned face down. Throughout the song rehearsal, make sure they turn the song sheet face down on a regular basis — the purpose of the rehearsal is to memorize the song.

As with rehearsing dialog scenes, take time to explain meanings of any words, especially words that may be unfamiliar, colloquial, or allusions. Again and again, ask, "What's a poison pen/acid tongue/masquerade?"

You may need to explain jokes or puns. Many youngsters simply don't have the vocabulary to understand some jokes, the historical background to understand some references, or the musical knowledge to understand some spoofs. For example they may not know the song, "I Enjoy Being a Girl," which is the basis of humor in the song, "I Enjoy Being a Ghoul" in *Phantom of the Op'ry*. In these cases, you need to explain the jokes or even play the original number.

After they have chanted the stanza and learned any vocabulary necessary to understand it, the group should sing through the stanza a couple of times, first looking at the words, and then turning the song sheet face down. In this way, they learn the words and you can hear if they are hitting the right notes, getting the correct rhythm, and pronouncing words correctly.

Throughout their singing, always make positive comments after they sing each stanza, such as "Brilliant," "Excellent," "Well done," "Fantastic," "Beautiful," "Lovely." This will help them keep singing with concentration.

If the song has eight stanzas, teach the first four, then the last four, and then work on all eight together. In teaching the first four, once they seem to have the hang of stanza 1, work on stanza 2. Then sing stanzas 1 and 2 together. Then teach stanza 3 and sing stanzas 1, 2, and 3 together. Once they learn stanza 4, sing stanzas 1 to 4 together. Then start teaching stanzas 5 to 8.

If a song has several similar stanzas, or similar lines within stanzas, such as those in "Thank You Very Much" from *Scrooge*, try to help your singers to remember the correct order. For example, in "Thank You Very Much," the song mentions the bugle first, then the trumpet, then the cannon. As they start singing without the scripts, mime these different objects as they are mentioned in the song. Another useful technique is to know the order of the first word of each stanza. For example, have them memorize the first word of each of the seven stanzas of Bill Sykes' "My Name."

131

Once the group knows the words, start working with them on expression, dynamics, meanings, and of course, the right notes and rhythm. Singers will benefit from an extra dose of coaching if they need to come in on cues from other cast members — for example, the opening "I Enjoy Being a Ghoul" number in *Phantom of the Op'ry* or the chorus singing "Consider Yourself" along with the Artful Dodger in *Oliver*. Be sure to hand those songs over to your musical director when you have a music-only rehearsal.

Of course, once you start adding in dance steps, the pace, dynamics, and meaning you have established during the singing rehearsals will temporarily go out the window, but you will easily recapture it once the group learns the movements.

A final tip: Select someone to be the "lead singer" for each group number. This can be a principal if a principal is the main singer in a group song, or a strong chorus member. You may want two people, perhaps one on each side of the stage if the group is large. These singers are responsible for taking the lead in starting the song, and then the others can follow them.

Common signals for conducting singers

There are no standard signals or arm movements, only what is, in retrospect, common sense. Here are some suggestions:

- To signal increased volume, raise arm, palm upward.
- To signal decreased volume, lower arm, palm downward.
- To signal that the singers cannot be heard, cup your hand to your ear and screw up your face.
- To indicate they need to take a big breath, point to your diaphragm.
- To show they need to hold a note, move hand slowly up and out.
- To show the note needs to be stopped, lift hand and snatch it back.
- To signal to a group or soloist to come in, point to them and raise arm, palm upward.
- To signal to a group or soloist to stop or reduce volume, point to them and lower arm, palm downward.

One common tricky situation is where singers come in at different times. You need to signal to whoever needs to come in next. Simultaneously, you need to motion to the rest of the group either to stop singing or to quiet down so the new voice can be clearly heard.

Coaching singers for a better performance

Here are some typical coaching tips that you may find helpful in a number of singing situations:

"Take a breath here."

"Hold that note."

"Make the words clearer."

"Think about the words! What mood are you in as you sing this song?"

"Clap the rhythm!"

"Listen to the music here. Follow the tune."

Have them repeat a particular section once or twice only. Then have them do the entire song again. Ignore any impulse you may feel to "drill" a section over and over. Such intense practice seldom improves the scene and it turns the kids off.

To help singers project their voices and achieve a rounded sound, have them think of their mouths, noses, and faces as their musical instruments when it comes to singing. Simply blowing air though the big hole in their face (their mouths) does not produce good sound. They must also sing out through their noses and the sound must vibrate through their cheeks and foreheads, which act as speakers.

By singing out through their noses, not just their mouths, the singers produce not a nasal twang, but the best sound possible, caused by air vibrating over the membranes. Ask them to think about someone whistling or any wind instrument being played — it's not just a matter of force, the air has to be shaped and controlled. So while they are singing, advise your singers:

"Feel the vibrations in your cheeks!"

"Push the sound through your nose!"

"Imagine you have two speakers in your forehead!"

"Imagine your ears are speakers!"

"Let the song come through your forehead!"

Using a vocal accompaniment track in teaching songs

During your first singing rehearsals, when you are learning the song without any choreography, use an accompaniment track with words included. The recorded voices are usually highly professional and very adult sounding, and your group may be somewhat hesitant to join in. Set an example and join in yourself. Shout out lots of encouragement to get all the singers to sing along and, if possible, drown out the recorded voice. Repeat this several times, usually over one or two rehearsals, until the group sings along with the recording confidently and follow the dynamics of the song, perhaps getting louder or softer in appropriate sections. Once the group sings confidently on their own, you should stop singing, although you will probably need to mouth the words along with the singers.

Once the group seems to know the words of the song and understands the meaning, you are ready to the start using the part of the accompaniment track that does not have words, or to stop using the recording altogether. The first time they sing the song without the benefit of a recorded voice, sing along with the group. The next time, mouth the words at them. Have the group establish the beat.

Use the signals described earlier to indicate when the dynamics change. Help the group establish the mood and energy — instruct them to smile brightly if they are singing an exuberant song or look serious during a somber or anxious number.

Getting the most from music rehearsals

If your musical director is not available for every rehearsal, you will have certain rehearsals devoted to rehearsing and polishing musical numbers. See the sample thirty-six-week rehearsal schedule in chapter 3 for more details. To get the most from these music rehearsals, be ready to present your music director with a list of "problem areas" in singing that have cropped up during your own rehearsals. As you teach the songs and work through them, make notes of any passages that repeatedly present difficulties to your group. When you do have a music rehearsal, present your list of problem areas to the musical director, and ask that they get extra attention and practice.

As a rule, children experience problems if the song does not follow a consistent pattern, demands anything other than everyone singing exactly the same thing at the same time, or has complex harmonies. For example, during the song, "Luck Be a Lady Tonight," in *Guys and Dolls*, the chorus needs to sing completely different words from the principal but at the same time. Either Sky, the chorus, or both parties have difficulty singing what are essentially two different songs at the same time.

Another typical example is the chorus of the song "Tomorrow" from *Annie*. The final crescendo, "You're always a day away" has the same words, but not the same tune. In the first two repetitions of this line, the last three notes go down, but in the last repetition, the three notes go up and are held. Children tend either to forget to go up on the third time, or they start going up during the second chorus instead of waiting for the third. They also tend to forget to take a big breath in preparation for the held notes in the third chorus.

Tips for preparing actors to perform with an accompaniment track

An accompaniment tape or CD is an inexpensive and convenient way to provide musical accompaniment. As long as your CD or tape player works, you face no scheduling problems or live musicians. The main challenge is that the actors may struggle to keep exact pace with the recording. Unlike a live pianist, an accompaniment track cannot accommodate any missteps or changes from the singers.

Because an accompaniment track sets a rhythm and cannot react if your group unexpectedly leaves out the second stanza, you need to rehearse the songs often and carefully. Keep some of the following points in mind:

- Don't add any dance steps until the group sings along with the accompaniment track properly, including appropriate expression and dynamics.
- For each song, practice repeatedly exactly *when* the group needs to come in with the accompaniment track. Normally there will be a short instrumental introduction before the singing actually begins.
- When you first teach the song, use the version with the voice recording. Ask the group to listen carefully to the instrumental music that is played before the singing begins. Ask the group to hum along with the instrumental section, perhaps counting out the beat, so they have a very precise sense of when the solo instrumentation ends and their singing joins in; getting this timing right is the first big step in using an accompaniment track with success.
- To help your singers come in on time, give them visual cues. First, as the instrumentation ends, give the singers a cue to draw a breath. Then give them another visual cue to start

singing. Later, during dress rehearsals and performances, you or your musical director will give the group these cues from an inconspicuous place in the front of the audience.

• Once they begin singing, the group must keep pace with the accompaniment track, pause for any instrumental interludes to be played, and again come in on cue with the music. Keeping pace is the second big step in using an accompaniment recording, so rehearse the songs until the correct pace is achieved. Then work on the dynamics and expression of the song, and then add the dancing.

• Emphasize that the singers must *listen to* and *follow the music.*

Choreography

The role of the choreographer

For most shows, it isn't necessary that a trained dancer choreograph every number. Most of your performers are unlikely to have had dance training and are unlikely to be capable of terribly complicated moves. If you are totally inexperienced in this area and are uncertain whether you can develop and run dance sequences, read through the rest of this section, where you will find numerous ideas and tips for choreographing young performers.

Choose a dance number from the show and try to work out some movements that would work with your group. Then decide if you still need a full-time choreographer for your show. You might want to use an experienced choreographer for any special solo numbers, but try, if possible, to work out most group numbers yourself. Big dance numbers are the most memorable part of most musicals and need lots of rehearsal and coaching, so the more of it you can do yourself, the more flexibility and control you will have.

Choreography and young performers

Song and dance numbers should serve to advance the story in the song and plot in the script. Choreography should produce an extended expression of the meaning of the song that neither takes a "paint by numbers" approach nor produces a dance whose connection with the song's lyrics is perplexing at best.

In planning dance numbers for your group, keep in mind that in many cases, your performers will be expected to sing and dance at the same time, which is a surprisingly demanding task, rather like patting your head and rubbing your stomach at the same time. Try to provide as much simplicity and consistency as possible, which will help your players remember the routines and perform them with confidence. For example, try to make each different number as definitive and unique as possible, but use lots of repetition within each number.

In general, an audience finds watching simple, definite, well executed moves far more pleasing than enduring a complex routine of steps that the performers simply cannot manage with precision

Matching costumes enhance the visual appeal of simple choreography.

and grace. There is nothing more satisfying than watching everyone on-stage do exactly the same thing at the same time — even if the action is as simple as turning one's head to the right and marching three steps in place.

Another consideration in planning choreography is the size of the stage. If you are working on a small stage and have twenty-five actors, your room for maneuvering is, quite literally, extremely limited, leaving you to work mostly with hand and head movements, not full body leaps and spins.

Try to get a sense of your group's dance and movement talent as soon as possible, especially if the group is new. During any group work and the auditions, observe who seems to have the strongest sense of movement. Make a mental note to give these performers sections of numbers to perform on their own or in small groups; they will find such work extends the challenge of the show for themselves, and it will increase the depth of the musical numbers.

Planning and developing dance sequences

A dance sequence is simply a collection of movements, done by specific performers at specific times in a particular order, rather like a gymnastics routine for twenty-five people.

The first step in developing a dance sequence is to become very familiar with the lyrics and music. Your performers will do a better job if the choreography is closely linked to what the lyrics are about. Listen to each song you will be choreographing over and over again.

As you listen, make sure you are clear about the sequence of the individual stanzas, refrain (chorus), and the instrumental sections.

Make a preliminary plan as to which performers will be dancing to which sections of the song — the entire chorus, or a few dancers only? Also, plan how the dancers will be grouped on-stage at the start of the dance, where they will move to during the dance, and where they end up.

We recommend that your dance numbers use the entire chorus as often as possible. This keeps them on the stage, where their family friends can see them, where they can learn dance skills, and where you can keep control of them.

In planning how you will group your performers, try to achieve as much artistic consistency and repetition as you can; this will help the players remember the dances and perform them with confidence. This approach also simplifies your task because it reduces the number of decisions you need to make in planning each routine.

It helps your performers if they start every dance number from the same place on-stage, or at least from the same side of the stage. From their point of view, it's much easier to remember that, "If it's a dance, go down stage left," than to keep seven different locations in mind. You will also save yourself from twenty kids asking you simultaneously, "Where do I stand?"

It is usually easier on your performers if you start off on the same foot each time; for example, always move the right foot first. This consistency and simplicity is very helpful to the actors when they perform before an audience and are feeling nervous and excited.

If there are lots of numbers with partners, as in *Guys and Dolls*, try to arrange for dancers to have the same partner throughout the show. From the point of view of your actors, it's much easier to remember *who* your partner is if it's the same for each number. Having the same partner also improves the chances of the pair becoming used to each other's moves.

Also, in planning your arrangement of performers on-stage, keep in mind that they all need to see each other as much as possible to keep their movements synchronized. Try to accommodate the different heights of the performers and the need for the audience (particularly parents) to see them as fully as possible. Taller performers generally should be placed at the back of the stage, while the shorter performers are in the front. This can contradict the needs of your younger, less confident performers, who usually want to watch and follow someone else during dance routines. If they are all at the front of the stage, they can only see the audience and panic sets in. One solution is to place two of your taller, older, more savvy performers downstage right and left, where they don't block the view, but where the younger, smaller performers can still watch and follow them when necessary.

To increase artistic consistency, actors can use the same gesture or movement each time they sing a particular phrase. For example, they can lift their arm the same way each time they sing the words, "Consider yourself," or "Doing what comes naturally," or "I enjoy being a ghoul." This has the added benefit of requiring actors to remember only one gesture or movement each time they sing that particular line.

Indeed, plan for the players to perform the same routine each time they sing the refrain or chorus stanza to a song. This repetition helps the movement to reflect the meaning of the refrain, which after all, is the same each time. To keep things from being too repetitious, perhaps choreograph them to move to a new position on-stage during the other stanzas. Alternatively, have them repeat the same set of steps, but face downstage right the first time, downstage left the second time, and full front the last time. This way, the children have to learn to remember only a single routine for a single set of lyrics. It's actually quite difficult to associate different sets of movements, and to perform them in the correct order, to the same set of lyrics.

For the different unrepeated lyrics in a song, you may want to use the group of performers you have identified as having specific dance talent while others stand to one side or behind them. Or you may want to use the entire on-stage cast, but divide them into smaller groups and have each perform one set of lyrics.

Instrumental sections present another good opportunity to showcase your more talented dancers while the others stand to one side, perhaps doing hand movements. Instrumental sections require that performers can remember a fixed dance routine without having the extra help that lyrics provide in remembering what to do when. When no song is being sung, dancing talent — or lack of it — becomes extremely apparent. You need to use either very simple movements during an instrumental section or your best dancers.

As you listen to the song, think about movements that do the following:

• Support the meaning of the song
• Look effective from the audience's point of view
• Can be performed — and remembered — by your group

If the movements reflect the meaning of the song and underscore current mood and action of the show, the song will be more memorable to the audience. The performers will also have a far easier time remembering what they need to do — no small feat when they have six or seven songs to learn and perform.

At the same time, avoid slavish mimicry, which looks foolish. For example, if while singing "I See the Moon," the children first point to their right eyes ("I"), then put a hand above the eyebrows and gaze at the audience ("see"), and then point straight upwards ("the moon"), they will simply look silly. However, a smooth upward sweep of the hand, ending in an open palm towards the ceiling, expresses the line's meaning, is easy to execute, and looks elegant on stage.

As you listen to the song, aim to select a few effective movements and arrange them into different patterns. You do not need to think up one hundred different movements for each song; it is far better to use ten movements, repeated in different patterns during the course of a song. This pattern of repeated movements works to build a symmetry and consistency between the different parts of the songs; watching the pattern emerge provides immense satisfaction to the audience. Remember, the fewer the movements, the simpler your task.

Try to select movements that your group can perform flawlessly. In our experience, the best movements are simple movements, perfectly performed by everyone on-stage at the same time. You can usually succeed in getting thirty people to turn their heads to the right, but thirty people spinning twice usually results in three perfect pirouettes and twenty-seven wobbly, unsteady turns that match nothing else being done on-stage — in short, a vision of chaos. See the following section for ideas for finding movements that children can successfully perform.

Finally, as you listen to the songs, establish the rhythm, which is usually 1-2, 1-2-3, or 1-2-3-4. See if the rhythm changes during the number. Feel the beat and clap out the rhythm. Have a firm idea of how many bars are in each section, because that will control the number of movements that can be performed. See if the tempo, or the pace of music changes during the song; the performer's movements will need to accommodate any changes. If you are uncertain, seek advice from your musical director.

Selecting movements

In collecting ideas for movements, you may find it helpful to watch any film or video versions of the show. Indeed, watching dance sequences in any musical performed by live actors will help spark your own ideas and build your confidence as a choreographer. Just keep in mind that your performers may not be able to execute all the complex steps that the professionals in these shows can do. Do take care not to copy any exact sequence of dancing, to avoid any possible plagiarism.

Another good source of ideas for dance sequences is the group itself. A useful activity during the audition phase — or at any time — is to divide the players into teams of six to eight, and ask them to devise a dance to a song. See the section, "Movement and dance auditions," in chapter 7 for full details. This exercise is also useful because it demonstrates what your group is capable of doing.

As the groups perform their dances, watch carefully for good bits that might be incorporated into the show itself. If you do adopt something, an immensely popular move is to christen it after the actor who thought it up or the group who first performed it. If you ask the group to please do the "Kimberly hula hoop bit" or the "Alice step," you will show that you take their ideas seriously, not to mention putting big smiles on Kimberly and Alice.

Another source of ideas is to look at the historic setting of the show and the specific setting of each number within the show. The 1920s and 30s, the setting for *Annie* and *Bugsy Malone,* were awash with specific, signature dances such as the Charleston; turn of the century Russia, the setting for *Fiddler on the Roof*, would be a place of folk dances. On the other hand, the long dresses in *Oliver* might affect the movements you choose for "Who Will Buy?" Keep in mind the actual setting and characters of a particular number. In *Annie*, the dance steps performed by adult servants in a mansion would differ from those performed by young orphans in a children's home.

Some general tips about choosing dance steps are as follows:

• Children respond well to marching movements, and find them easy to remember. You can create pleasant and effective patterns on the stage by having the performers changing a marching movement to a new direction. For example, the children begin in three lines, marching in place, all facing to the right; have the first, then the second and finally the third line reverse direction and march to the left; then have them form columns that face the audience. The "Be Back Soon" song from *Oliver* works well with this approach.

• Pat-a-cake type movements are good to use with younger performers. The actors work with a partner, which provides a feeling of security, and they don't have to move their feet, which simplifies their task. For variations, they can slap right and left hands with each other, both hands with each other, slap their knees, and clap their own hands together. They can switch places with another pair or with each other between stanzas to increase movement and interest.

• It is always safe to develop a routine where the actors remain standing in one place, but use head, arm, and leg movements.

• Grapevine or chain movements are usually a safe choice. When coaching them, shout "change" when they need to move to the next person. If someone is missing during a rehearsal, that person becomes "Mr. Nobody."

• Spins and 360s are two movements that don't work with groups, although solo performers may be able to execute them impeccably.

As you listen to the song in the privacy of your home or empty classroom, execute your chosen movements. Check that their rhythm fits with the rhythm of the song. Remember that you need to plan and allow time for "movements" that simply allow the actors to change the direction they are facing or change from one foot to another. Finally, if you can't do the movements easily, there is probably no hope for your group of young performers. Find another movement.

Recording dance movements

In developing your movements, you need to record them, in pencil, on the musical score. Otherwise you will forget them, no matter how memorable they may seem when you first create them. Penciling them onto the score is essential because it provides you a place to record dance steps when no words are being sung.

Unlike musical notes, there is no standard method of dance notation. Some organizations have attempted to introduce standard dance notation systems, although they tend to be aimed at professional choreographers and may seem complex for your needs. Information about these organizations is given in Appendix 2 — Resources.

However, you will naturally develop your own system of notation as you develop your dance sequences. Here are some tips:

- If you have had any dance training yourself, some of the terminology may help you, such as "heel-toe, toe-heel," "first position, second position," and so forth.
- Remember that left and right need to be from the performers' point of view as they face the audience.
- Assume that most of the kids will have *no* knowledge of dance terminology. They are usually quite happy to learn it if you take the time to teach it.
- Use abbreviations for commonly used words and characters. Make a master list of these in the front of your script. Use the common stage abbreviations such as UL, DR, R, L, and FF. You will also end up with a vast set of dance-related terms and abbreviations — for example, Stp = step, Stmp = stamp, Tp = tap.
- Drawing stick figures above the bars in the music score can be helpful to show arm and leg movements.
- Arrows can be useful to show turns or movements. For turns, include the degree (for example, 90°, 180°) and the direction of the turn (left or right). For movements, an up or down arrow can have numerous meanings; you can label variations with

specific notes, such as "Turn to face audience" or "Turn away from audience."

• A bird's-eye-view sketch of the stage can show starting positions and changes in position on the stage. It is helpful to have one of these at the beginning of each staff or stanza, so you can easily see where everyone is at given moments of the number.

Teaching dance sequences

When teaching the movements to the group, first demonstrate the movements on-stage as the song plays and the group watches you. Then teach the dance. The group needs to be on their feet, either on the stage or in another rehearsal area. It is very difficult to learn — or to teach — movements while translating "right to left." To teach the dance, stand with your back to the players so they can follow your movements easily.

For the following example, assume that each stanza is four lines long. You will help the group learn each line separately, then build up to the whole stanza, then groups of stanzas, and finally the entire song. The aim of your "dance rehearsal" is for the players to perform the whole dance from memory, without stopping.

1. Go through the movements of the first line of the first stanza on its own, *chanting* the song, with the group mimicking you. Repeat.
2. Do the same with second line on its own, with the group mimicking you. Repeat. Do the first and second lines together, one after another. Repeat.
3. Do the third line on its own, with the group mimicking you. Repeat. Do lines 1, 2, and 3 together, one after another. Repeat.
4. Do the fourth line on its own, with the group mimicking you. Repeat. Do lines 1–4 (the first stanza) together. Repeat. Then move on to the second stanza.
5. Do the fifth line on its own. Repeat.
6. Do the sixth line on its own. Repeat. Do lines 5 and 6 together.
7. Do the seventh line on its own. Repeat. Do lines 5, 6, and 7 together. Repeat.
8. Do the eighth line on its own. Repeat. Do lines 5–8 (the second stanza) together. Do both stanzas (lines 1–8) together. Repeat.

9. Continue through the entire song, working a stanza at a time until they can perform the entire song without stopping.

As you take the group through the line-by-line chanting version of the song, give them very specific instructions. Be sure to indicate clearly whether you need them to move the *right* foot or the *left* leg. Some examples of clear instructions are:

"Right hand moves to right."

"Head turns right."

"Head looks forward."

"Right hand to stomach."

"Wait two beats."

"Snap left fingers."

"Tap left heel."

Every once in while, sneak a look behind you and see if any of the movements are too complex for the entire group to do smoothly. You will be surprised to find that a movement you consider simple will send many of your performers sprawling on the floor. If a movement is too complex, you can either simplify the dance, or have your best dancers dance the steps while the rest of the group sings along.

Learning the steps is tricky, so be patient with your group. In addition, some of the your dancers will find it difficult simply to remember *what comes next*. To help them, when you repeat the entire sequence, repeat and emphasize the links between one stanza and the next. For example: "Now left foot forward. [During slight pause in music:] From left foot forward, right foot back. Now both feet together. Then bounce up and down."

Never be afraid to change a movement. Just be very firm and definite in all your instructions. Simply announce, "I'm changing this!" or "We are no longer doing that!" If you have a new idea between sessions, don't hesitate to try it out.

As always, use lots of superlatives as your group works through the sequence, no matter how chaotic things may appear to you. After each set of moves, words like "Great work," "Fabulous," "Super," "Stupendous," and "Wonderful," work wonders to keep your group motivated and to keep trying. Your group will also appreciate the occasional wry remark, such as "OK, let's see how terrible this looks."

Expect, in some instances, to have to lead one or two performers personally through the steps before they catch on. Alternatively, you can ask one of your more experienced dancers to do so. Some people need to repeat the steps a few more times and then the sequence sinks in.

Keep repeating your instructions and words of encouragement. Eventually the mayhem will end and your group will be performing the dance steps all by themselves. They will roundly — and rightly — congratulate themselves on their achievement. Learning a dance sequence, as anyone who does line or country dancing can tell you — is a wonderful experience.

Once the group seems to have grasped it, go through the entire sequence without stopping.

Practicing dance sequences in rehearsal

No matter how carefully you have taught the dances, and no matter how quickly your group may have learned them, when it comes to rehearsing them a few weeks later, don't be discouraged if all your efforts seemed to have been for naught. You will announce, "Now let's run through 'Consider Yourself,'" and your performers will look at you blankly.

This is where your notes come in handy. Direct them to their places, with lots of "Remember, you are over here with Jane." Direct them to chant the song while they work through the steps, which you may have to recall for them. This will get them back on track so they can actually start singing and dancing the number.

Once they have grasped the dance routine, work on any group entrances and exits. There may be too many to come on all at once. Practice coming in and going off, following in the order they stand on-stage, and not making a mad dash for their assigned places at the start of the dance or for off-stage at the end of the dance.

As they practice the dance at each rehearsal, coach them to perform movements clearly and concisely, with definite beginnings and endings. Encourage your performers to do their dance movements big and bold or not at all, just as with acting. It also adds energy to the performance if they look up — not at their feet — and always *smile* when dancing.

Preparing Musical Accompaniment

Accompaniment track

If you are using an accompaniment track for musical accompaniment, you simply need to make sure that the CD or tape stays intact during the rehearsal period, and that the CD is always in the case when you move it from place to place. If the hall you plan to use has a PA or sound system, make sure it works. If you must provide your own system, just check that it is large enough for the size of the hall. Check the location of power outlets; you may need to bring an extension cable. The sound technician you use for other sound effects should be able to play the track on cue and adjust the volume occasionally. For more detailed information, see the section, "Integrating sound effects into the show," in chapter 12.

Live musical accompaniment

If you are using live music, you will need to recruit musicians and find musical instruments and any amplification equipment necessary for the hall you plan to use. How elaborate a band you want is, as usual, up to you. Check with the licensing arrangements to see if there is a minimum or maximum band size. Piano and percussion usually provide sufficient musical accompaniment.

Finding musicians

If you are working as a drama teacher at a school with a good performing arts program, you may be able to draft in band or orchestra students — and the band director — as your musicians and conductor. If you don't have access to a ready-made band, you need to find experienced musicians who can sight-read the score. If you are using only piano and percussion, the musical director may double as the pianist.

If you are working as a private group, someone may have a relative or friend interested in accompanying the show. If you cannot find any musicians through your group or other usual contacts, check with local churches, amateur groups, and music stores. Experienced musicians expect a fee, which may vary wildly.

If you are using paid musicians, the more you use them the more you pay, so seek to minimize the time you have them in rehearsals. Normally, if you have used recorded music for most of your rehearsals, you should be able to get away with using your musicians for one music rehearsal, the dress rehearsal, and the performances. See the sample thirty-six-week rehearsal schedule in chapter 3 for an example of when musicians need to be present.

Before you sign anyone up to play, whether for a fee or not, be sure to hear them and determine their actual musical ability. If you personally have no ear for music, have someone who does listen to them play. Finally, check and double-check the musician's availability for performances and rehearsals. Have a backup in mind if any accompanist becomes unexpectedly unavailable.

When you agree to use a musician, check that they will provide their own instruments, or know of a source. Pianists normally will expect a piano to be available at the venue, although keyboardists may have their own. Again — we cannot stress the following point enough — always double-check that your venue will have a piano available on the rehearsal and performance dates you need it, and that the piano is tuned.

Incorporating live music into the performance

If you are using paid musicians, book them for the last three rehearsals and the performances only. If you are using a free resource, such as the school orchestra, try to get them to come to earlier run-throughs. They may not be willing to donate much more time.

At some point before the rehearsal with live musicians, you need to meet with them if they are a small group or their director if they are a large group, to discuss the score and libretto in detail. In particular do the following:

• Point out any cuts or other changes to the libretto or score.

• Explain where you need a musical bridge between actions or scenes, or any vamping (repetition of bars) while actors enter or exit, or when scenery is changed.

• Explain any changes in volume — cues for them to fade out music and then stop; start music softly, and then increase volume; decrease volume during solos and duets; increase volume during big dance scenes without singing, and so forth.

• Explain any visual cues that are actions or entrances; for example, "Jed leaves, and Nellie turns and shrugs her shoulders and walks downstage toward the microphone."

As far as rehearsing the musicians with the show, the musical director, if you have one, will put the musicians and singers through their paces. If not, as you go through the show, discuss the tempo of each number with the conductor and let the musicians play a bit of it. Then ask the actors to sing along while the musicians play until it feels the right speed and the actors are comfortable with the sound, which will seem unfamiliar after rehearsing with a recording. Check that the music does not drown out the children's voices, and if necessary, try to get the musicians to control the volume.

Chapter 11

Preparing Scenery, Props, and Costumes

"Production" vs. Performance

The design, production, and organization of scenery, props, lighting, sound, costumes, and makeup can be a huge task in addition to getting the performers ready to perform. It's important to keep the "production" from overpowering the energy of the performance.

In our experience, most drama group members tend to have a short-lived interest in production. The actual work of painting scenery, making props, or organizing costumes is often beyond the patience and diligence of most youngsters. A production does not need elaborate staging, but it does require energetic and enthusiastic performers.

However, some production matters need attention. Props and costumes can help the actors build character, and are sometimes important to the plot itself. Sounds effects can be crucial to the plot. Doorbells or phones ringing must occur on cue. If a video of the show is available, watching it can give you ideas of costumes, scenery, props, and sound.

In our own productions, we tend to concentrate on preparing the performers, and take a "minimalist" approach to technical matters. Sometimes we are fortunate enough to have an energetic parent who enjoys helping us put on an elaborate show. You will have your own preferences.

This book gives a broad overview of the technical requirements of musicals. It does not go into detail about any aspect of technical production, such as costuming, prop-making, scenery construction, lighting design, or sound effects. However, there are numerous books, reference materials, courses, and other resources available to help you to develop your own skills in these areas, or to provide information on a particular historic period or construction technique. See Appendix 2 — Resources. Here you will also find information about finding suppliers and rental agencies for costumes, scenery, properties, lighting, sound equipment, and sound effects.

If you decide to design and make an elaborate set, costumes, or lighting plan, make sure you have the commitment and organization from your group (or their parents) to support your efforts. Recruit help from the parents and family members; often someone in the group has a brother or sister who is not interested in attending the workshops, but who will quite happily paint scenery or run lights during final rehearsals and performances.

Schedule additional sessions for costume making, scenery building, painting, flameproofing, and light-rigging so the scenery and other effects are ready in time — at the very latest, for the technical rehearsal. These sessions need to be planned meticulously so everyone has something to do and all the tools necessary for the job are available.

Costumes

Costumes are an instant visual clue to character, and also help the actors feel "in character." Watch the video, if available, for ideas of costumes, keeping in mind that most Hollywood budgets far exceed your own. If a list of costumes has been provided with the script, go through it to see what is absolutely essential. If no list has been provided, go through the script to determine what costumes are required. Check the historical period in which the play takes place and refer to a reference book on fashion for accuracy.

In addition to developing your own master list, once rehearsals get underway, ask your actors to compile their own list of the costumes that their character or characters will need. This exercise helps them understand the show and may even inspire them to suggest a way of getting the costume. Alternatively, leave out some lists for them to complete, with columns for Character/Scene/ Costume/Props. See figure 13 for a sample chart.

List all characters that you play, and describe what costumes they wear and when:			
Character	**Scenes**	**Costumes**	**Prop**
Orphan	night	nightgown	teddy bear blanket
	day	old dress, old shoes	rag doll
Servant	1st	black dress or skirt/top, white apron	duster
	2nd	same	tea tray, 2 tea cups, tea pot
Boylan Sister	Show scene	glittery dress, wig, silver shoes, glittery tights	lipstick and handbag

Figure 13 – Sample costume chart for cast to complete

Obtaining costumes

In planning the budget for your show, you need to decide how you are going to obtain the costumes if you do not already have them on hand. It is wise to tell the parents, ideally on the flyer about your group, whether the performers will be expected to provide costumes and other items, or if there will be any charges to the parents for costumes. Don't let a situation arise where you are facing an angry parent who assumed all costumes would be included within the course fees because they were given no information to the contrary.

Group members providing their own costumes

In any case, for most roles, you can usually ask the group members to provide their own costumes. This reduces the cost of production and gets the performers involved. Make sure the parents receive a clear, written description of what their child or children require and issue it at least one month before the first dress rehearsal. They may want to raid the thrift stores or charity shops or borrow things from an uncle in the next town.

The easiest method for providing this information is to draw up a full costume list for the entire show. Your script may include such a list. Write down the name of each character, or group of characters, such as "orphans" or "people in nightclub." You may want to distinguish further between "boys in nightclub" and "girls in nightclub."

Below each character name, list every costume to be used and its source if you do not expect the performers to provide it themselves. For example, the item "golden top hat" might be annotated as "to be provided." Along with the costumes, list any personal props, such as the metal buckets and wooden scrub brushes in *Annie*, the wooden bowls and spoons in *Oliver*, or the dice and cards in *Guys and Dolls*.

On the list you send home, try to include detailed, specific information about any color and style required. This will help the performers and parents acquire the correct items, and may save your nineteenth-century orphans from wearing shirts decorated with multinational logos. For example, your list could include detailed information as follows:

- Socks: plain black, gray, brown, or dark blue, ankle or calf height.
- Shoes: plain lace-up or slip-on leather or leather-look black, dark blue, or brown, *not* sneakers, running shoes, or trainers
- At least *two* ponytail bands or baubles, any bright color, any style

The list is also an appropriate place to indicate if you are able to obtain any items at a volume discount. This gives the parents the option of either providing the costume themselves or paying you for it. An example of this situation is providing gangster hats in either *Guys and Dolls* or *Bugsy Malone*. You can usually get these at a discount from a costume supply shop or possibly from a wholesaler

Gangsters wear hats, suit coats, and ties brought from home or purchased at a thrift store.

if you can find one. The parents then simply pay you for the individual hat, which of course the performer gets to keep. This process is convenient and often cheaper for the parents and results in a matching set of hats.

Finally, on the list indicate which costumes you expect to collect immediately after the show, such as the costumes that have been rented or properties from the group collection. You can even ask that items, like shirts, be laundered after the show and returned at the final workshop.

Make copies of this full list for each cast member. On each copy, write the actor's name and highlight or circle the names of the all the characters that apply to the individual performers; many will be playing several roles.

Buying, borrowing, renting, and making costumes

For character roles, you may need to buy, borrow, rent, or make costumes. If you have the time to make a round of the thrift stores or charity shops in your area, they can often supply costumes, such as suits and hats, at low cost. This is a good time to call on parents or even grandparents for help — some people positively enjoy trawling through local church sales and garage sales for prize items and will bring you back a wealth of props and costumes.

For borrowing costumes, the best sources are local amateur dramatic societies and schools. Some dramatic societies have a policy of charging for the use of costumes, but this cost may be less than that levied by a commercial rental shop.

If you need a particularly complicated or unusual costume, or one fashioned from fabric that would cost a fortune to buy, consider hiring or renting it. Provide clear sizing information, especially height, to the rental company. Some costumes may be sized for adults. Because your adolescent actors may experience a growth spurt over the course of a long rehearsal period, hold off providing exact size information until the last possible moment.

Do expect some unsolicited contributions from your group. Normally, by the second rehearsal, you will have someone at your elbow with the observation, "I have this red dress ... " Obviously, the actress is dying to wear it on-stage. Stay noncommittal at this point. You can either hope the performer will eventually forget this item, or you can ask her to bring it in and then either reject or accept it as being consistent with the style or historical period of the show.

If you decide to make some of the costumes, you can usually find, from a workshop group of thirty, about one or two parents who are willing and able to make some costumes. Be sure to reimburse any costs of fabric, patterns, or thread that you do not provide to them.

For more resources on making your own costumes, see Appendix 2 — Resources.

Makeup

For most characters, makeup isn't necessary and we don't recommend it unless you have an adult helper who is willing to oversee its use — and putting it away — before the dress rehearsal and each show. Although the kids may love it, it's messy, and there are many other things going on just before the show starts. Because eye infections can be easily spread by sharing makeup, each child ideally needs to have his or her own supplies, which also complicates things.

Even when your performers are playing elderly people, they will be more successful in portraying their characters if they concentrate on body language, pace, voice, and costume instead of depending on a few lines drawn on their faces. Many of your chorus members will be playing several roles and really won't have time, along with their speedy costume changes, to put on new makeup.

One exception to this advice are female characters like the Hot Box dancers in *Guys and Dolls* or the girls in Fat Sam's Speakeasy in *Bugsy Malone*. They can put on rouge, lipstick, and eyeliner at home before they come, with their parents' help. Simply add this requirement to the costume list for them.

If, despite the reservations expressed here, you are enthusiastic about using makeup, there are many books and other helps to get you started. See Appendix 2 — Resources.

Scenery and Furniture

Scenery and furniture, like other aspects of production, can be as elaborate or as simple as you wish. If you have a large stock of backdrops, furniture, set pieces, and platforms (rostrums) already available, you may need virtually nothing. Review the script and judge what is essential to the plot. Whatever on-stage effects you hope to achieve, check your storage capabilities. If you are renting a venue, will they allow you to store scenery and furniture for weeks on end? If not, where will you keep it?

When planning for furniture, try to be consistent. If you are on a tight budget, use your folding tables and plastic chairs with no apologies. What can look silly is to have a mix of vintage and institutional furniture in the same scene.

When working with the stage crew or anyone who will be moving anything bulky or heavy, make sure they are strong enough and that they know how to lift and move items safely. See section, "Lifting and handling objects safely," in chapter 14.

A minimalist approach

If you have absolutely no budget, use the bare or curtained stage with folding tables and plastic chairs and put your energies into creating the best performance possible. If you have a small amount of money, you can get by with very little and still mount a credible show. Here is a sample minimalist setting for *Annie*:

Young actors don't need elaborate scenery to shine.

- One backdrop of '30s New York City
- One or two desks for Warbucks and Miss Hannigan, used on opposite sides of the stage
- Enough rostrums (platforms) to extend across the back of the stage. (The size of each and total number will depend on the size of your stage area.)

The rostrums provide a variation in the levels for the chorus numbers, act as beds for the orphans, and become the stage for Bert Healey.

Assuming you have very little or nothing to start with, the following section suggests some options for pulling a set together.

Borrowing or renting scenery and furniture

Amateur theatre groups and schools may be willing to lend you scenery pieces, providing you do not need the same items on the same performance dates they do, and you feel confident you can return them in the same condition as they were in when you borrowed them. It may be difficult to get your insurance to pay for replacing borrowed items that you damage — check your policy and decide how much risk you are willing to carry. It is wise to take a conservative view — anything that can break, will.

If you have the money but little time or inclination to design, construct, paint, and store a set, there are suppliers who will deliver a set to your venue, or have it ready for collection if you have the appropriate vehicle and muscle power to pick it up. Simply check that the set you want is available for the time you want it, and reserve it. You receive dimensions, plans, and pictures to help you plan and rehearse prior to receiving the set.

The supplier should provide you scenery pieces and backdrops that conform to any local fire regulations you may need to meet. Check with your local requirements and with the supplier. Be certain to confirm that your facilities can accommodate the set provided. For example, you may need bars of a particular height for hanging backdrops.

Alternatively, you can also rent part of a set. For example, you can rent a single house for *Fiddler on the Roof*, a London backdrop for *Oliver*, or cars and the Speakeasy Bar for *Bugsy Malone*.

Large specific items of furniture, such as a roll-top desk for Scrooge, iron beds and an extra-large laundry basket for *Annie*, or a fancy dressing table for *Phantom of the Op'ry* can be hired or rented, usually from the same suppliers that rent backdrops and sets.

Buying or building your own

If you have the budget, design and construction talent, and storage space, you can build your own scenery and purchase your own furniture. This option gives you flexibility and the ability to create exactly what you want for your group. To justify the expense, buy or construct sets that can be used in a variety of shows in the future as well as this one.

157

The following list gives an overview of basic pieces that can be used for a variety of purposes.

Platforms (rostrums)

Collapsible, folding stage platforms or rostrums of varying sizes provide a flexible way of creating a number of scenic devices. Rostrums come as cubes or rectangular shapes of 2' x 2' x 2' or 3' x 2' x 2' and numerous other sizes. Some rostrums come as part of a modular system that has specific connecting devices that combine to make a safe and stable set.

Rostrums may be available at the performance venue or can be borrowed from theatrical groups or schools. They are a good investment if you have the money and storage space.

Rostrums can be used separately or pushed together to create beds (*Annie* or *Scrooge*), desks (*Annie*), tables (*Oliver*), bars (*Bugsy Malone*), or simply different stage levels. For large chorus scenes, rostrums at the back of the stage can raise the height of the children to a level where they are more visible to the audience. Another configuration is to put them into a horseshoe shape around the stage.

Rostrums are also helpful in extending the stage if you need more space, or creating a separate area in front of the stage. For example, in *Phantom of the Op'ry,* rostrums extending off the stage area can provide space for the two dressing rooms, leaving more space on-stage for the other scenes. In *Annie*, these extended areas can be used for solo numbers, such as Annie's "Tomorrow" or Bert Healey's "You're Never Fully Dressed Without a Smile." The same areas can also provide offices for Miss Hannigan and Daddy Warbucks.

The simple backdrop, newspaper stand, and mission sign effectively set the action of Guys and Dolls *in New York City.*

Backdrops

A backdrop, such as those described above, can be powerful in creating atmosphere at little cost. Just double-check that your venue has the bars to attach it to. You can then augment this backdrop with furniture and platforms (rostrums).

Materials for a backdrop are simple — canvas lengths

sewn together, hemmed at both top and bottom. You need to have some fittings at the top to attach it to the bar and a wide hem at the bottom for inserting a pole or other weight. You then need to find someone artistic who is willing to draw and paint the backdrop — this might be a cast member or parent, sibling or friend. Normally latex (emulsion) paint is sufficient as a medium. You may then need to flameproof the material by spraying it with the appropriate solution.

It is possible to project a scene onto the backdrop and paint it from the projected image. Alternatively, you can transfer a design through the use of a grid system. First sketch the backdrop design on a piece of paper or posterboard proportional to the size of the stage. Next, draw a grid over the sketch and larger, porportional grid on the backdrop cloth. Then transfer and enlarge the original drawing using the grid marks as a guide.

In addition to your unifying backdrop, a collection of platforms and furniture will offer a range of staging effects.

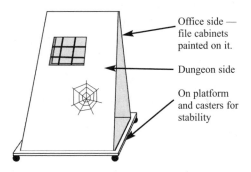

Office side — file cabinets painted on it.

Dungeon side

On platform and casters for stability

Figure 14a – A-frame

Set Pieces

If you have a handy parent or older sibling, you can create set pieces for your show. These add atmosphere and a sense of the era. The most useful set pieces are those that can fulfill two functions by turning them 180°. For example, for *Guys and Dolls*, one side can be the newspaper stand and the other side can be the Salvation Army altar. Another option is to make one side the exterior of a room or building and the other side the interior; for example, the exterior and interior of the mission in *Guys and Dolls*, the house in *Fiddler on the Roof,* or the orphanage in *Annie*.

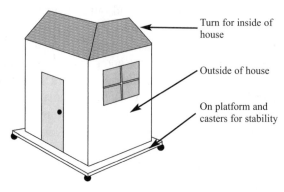

Figure 14b – L-shaped

A narrow *A-frame* of 2' x 2's can be mounted onto a 4' x 9' or 3' x 6' platform on casters that can be locked. Cover the frame with cardboard or canvas and paint as desired. See figure 14a.

Another way of creating a set piece is to paint the two sides of a *book flat*. A book flat is one that can stand by itself on end in a V or L shape. You can rent, buy, or make these flats yourself. Do make sure your actors don't accidentally knock them over. See figure 14b.

Tips on building scenery

If you plan to build and paint scenery, you need to schedule and plan the sessions to build it. Try to control who is in the group and keep the number of people involved fairly small and largely adult. Young kids — in fact, most kids — get bored very quickly after an initial burst of interest, often have no experience or skill in building and painting, and will need careful supervision. Also consider the following:

- Entice the group to complete the project with the promise of food at the end and drinks throughout. Bring a portable stereo so they can listen to music — either the musical or pieces of their choice.
- Make sure you have all your components and tools ready at the beginning of the session; it is all too easy to spend precious minutes and hours returning yet again to the building supply store to get mineral spirits, brushes, or nails.
- Depending on the local fire regulations, you may need to flameproof the scenery you build. Test the paint you plan to

use, and check that the flameproofer you spray on it doesn't make it run.

• Make sure you protect any curtains, floors, windows, and furniture by moving them out of the way and using plenty of drop cloths, old curtains, or sheets.

• Use water-based paint. Invest in the kind that won't run, even though it may cost a bit extra.

• Consider using a spray gun if you have a large area to cover.

• Allow time to clear things away and to clean up any sinks or floors that may be splattered with paint.

Evaluating the set as a whole

Once you have assembled your set, imagine it with the actors in costumes. If, at this point, you feel the overall effect is still too neutral, consider painting the rostrums, if you are using them, in a bright color to lend the set a bit more flair.

Keep in mind that with twenty to thirty children on the stage, only the top parts of the set and furniture will be seen. Also remember that most of the audience will be looking out for their children, grandchildren, and friends, not at the scenery, no matter how carefully it may have been designed and painted.

Props

The importance of props

Props are often important to the plot: money changes hands, a lapel rose squirts water; a locket is retrieved. They also help portray character. In *Grease*, Eugene and Patty's personalities are reflected in their books and clipboards.

An old-fashioned telephone adds interest and authenticity to this scene in Warbucks' office.

Buckets and mops announce the job titles of the cleaners in *Phantom of the Op'ry* and *Bugsy Malone*. The gangsters in *Bugsy Malone* and *Guys and Dolls* are immediately recognized by their dice, cards, guns, and rolls of money. The character of Lily St. Regis is reflected in her glittery handbag and her constantly used nail file. Nicely-Nicely's obsession with food is shown by his stash of food. Mr. Brownlow's age and social class are shown by his walking stick, ideally silver-topped.

Authentic-looking props can help compensate for a lack of extensive scenery. They lend extra texture and interest to a scene and make the action more accessable to both performer and audience. The jewels in *Oliver*, the hangman's noose in *Phantom of the Op'ry,* the buckets and mops in *Annie,* and the splurge guns in *Bugsy Malone* contribute to the story, character, and atmosphere.

If nothing else, props give performers something to do with their hands and help them develop stage business, which serves to emphasize character traits and enliven a scene for the audience.

If your script provides a list of props, double-check the action to make sure they are all listed. If no list is provided, go through the action and note every prop you will need. Making an initial list of props helps you to start planning how to obtain them and determine costs, if any.

In addition, ask your actors to compile their own lists of the props once rehearsals get underway. This exercise helps them to understand the show and to start thinking about what props their character might need or use as stage business. They may also give you ideas about how to get the property. If desired, have them fill out a chart similar to the one used for costumes earlier in this chapter.

Ways of obtaining props

Once you identify what you need, your options of obtaining them are similar to those for costumes and scenery.

Donations

This is obviously your best solution. As soon as the show is decided upon, it doesn't hurt to send home a list of props you will need, in hopes that someone just happens to have a locket, teapot, rotary telephone, lantern, or blanket they are about to throw out and would just as soon give to your group.

Borrowing

Simple non-breakable items can often be borrowed, ideally with the caveat that they may not be in the same pristine condition as when lent. Under no circumstances borrow any item of financial or sentimental value whose owner expects it to be returned in the same condition. Rehearsals and performances inflict massive wear and tear on props; they get dropped, thrown aside, or even stepped on in the darkness of backstage.

Renting

All sorts of things can be rented from theatrical suppliers —
from machine guns to milkmaids' yokes, from braziers to beer
barrels. Old-fashioned telephones or phonographs are typical, useful
items to rent.

Note for *Bugsy Malone* — budget extra cash for splurge guns
and foam. You tend to use more than you think you will.

Introducing props to the group

As properties start arriving for use in rehearsals, introduce them
to the cast and allow them all to have a chance to handle them as
they would be used in the play. Show them the swords, guns,
squirting flowers, wheeled flower cart, or any other properties
(especially if they produce noises or other effects), demonstrate how
to use them, and give them time to "play" with them. By doing this,
you satisfy the group's natural curiosity and they will tend to leave
things alone during the rehearsals and shows.

Chapter 12

Preparing Lighting and Sound

Lighting

Like all the other elements of your production, lighting can be as simple as it was in the time of the Greeks and Shakespeare — that is, *none* — or it can be elaborate as an Andrew Lloyd Webber production on Broadway or the West End. You will need to look at the budget, available equipment, technical help, and how much time you can devote to planning and executing your lighting scheme.

In general, lighting needs to do just that — light the action. If audience members cannot see the action, they become frustrated and restless. It's far more important to have enough lighting than to have special effects. Despite all the advantages and artistic satisfaction of a well lit show, lighting will not save a show that otherwise lacks focus, energy, and control. If all you have is overhead, general fluorescent lights, and they are bright enough to illuminate the actors, that will work fine.

Working around a lack of stage lighting

Because the typical modern script is often loaded with technical instructions about scenery and lighting, it may be helpful to review the purpose of lighting and put it into perspective against the overall effect of a show.

Here is a list of some of the main purposes of stage lighting, and some examples of how to work around a lack of lighting if that is what you face.

- Lighting creates mood and a sense of place and time. Whether the scene takes place during a moonlit night, on a bright sunny afternoon, in a dim alley, or at a garish nightclub, lighting can immediately help the audience establish a sense of place and atmosphere. However, costumes and props can provide much assistance in creating a mood and sense of a particular period. Acting can do the same. Emphasizing certain lines in the scene can also help; for example, "That sun is so bright today it hurts my eyes." Ultimately, the dialog delivery must establish mood — whether scary and frightened or boisterous and cheerful. At any rate, most lighting manuals recommend that special effects lighting be used only sparingly, at the beginning of a scene. The lights should then fade gradually into fuller lighting so the audience can still see the actors, who need to be acting the scene, not depending on lighting effects.

- Lighting may substitute for scenery. The use of accessories, such as color filters and gobos, can help to establish a mood and place, such as a jail cell or forest. If you lack elaborate lighting, use costumes and, of course, the acting itself to help establish location. The costumes of the maids or the finery of the lady of the house indicate a rich mansion. Coach the actors to emphasize lines that explain the time and location. Most of all, the performers need to *act* like maids who work in the mansion or like the lady of the house who calls the mansion home.

- Lighting helps with scene changes. A blackout signals the end of a scene, and darkness covers the mechanics of changing scenery. A scene can end on one side of the stage while another begins almost instantly on the other. You can create the same effect if the actors in the second scene are on-stage at the beginning, frozen in place, or enter quietly during the scene and then freeze into place. Once the group in the first scene finishes their lines, the second group begins their dialog. Meanwhile, the actors in the first group freeze in place or quietly leave the stage. You can also simply direct the second group to enter on cue and start their lines. Try different approaches and see which one works best.

- Through selective lighting, the audience's attention can be easily directed to a particular part of the stage, group of actors, or single performer; for example, when Oliver sings "Where Is Love?" or Annie sings "Tomorrow." If you have only general lighting, you can use actors' movements to help direct

165

attention. For example, the orphans can simply turn their backs and freeze while Annie sings "Tomorrow," as she moves closer to the audience. Or if an actor needs to deliver a soliloquy to the audience, the other actors can freeze in position.

• Lighting helps the audience be in two places at once — for example, Annie and Daddy Warbucks sing of their separate dilemmas, each lit up in a separate pool of light on either side of the stage; the Pink Ladies and the Greasers sing in their separate areas of the school. At the same time, lighting effects simply underscore what is already known — Daddy Warbucks and Annie do not, in fact, inhabit the same place; the Greasers and the Pink Ladies move in different worlds.

• Lighting increases the overall aesthetic satisfaction of watching a production; the "picture" on the stage has greater interest and depth because of the greater contrast in light and dark provided by stage lighting. However, the true aesthetics of a performance are in a good script, well acted. Your audience, which will be composed mostly of well-wishers, will forgive you for a lack of lights. What they won't suffer though is a boring, wilted performance by uninterested and uninteresting actors. What was good enough for the Greeks and the Elizabethans is surely good enough for the school musical.

That aside, if you have access to stage lighting, or are willing to pay for it, it does add to a show in all the ways mentioned above. So it is worth the effort to find out what you have available, and to decide how much more you want, and can afford, to add.

Assessing the available lighting at the venue

In planning your lighting, check what the venue provides. At one ideal extreme, the venue rental will include a wide range of appropriate, fully functioning lights and controls, complete with a technician fully trained to run them. At the other extreme, you will be operating in a fluorescent-lit school or church hall without a piece of lighting equipment in sight.

Sometimes the services of a technician are not included with the venue rental but can be obtained at an hourly rate. Sometimes the use of house technicians can be mandatory, even if charged at an extra cost — check whatever arrangements are in place.

If the venue does provide equipment and technicians, clarify roles and expectations as soon as possible. Here are some things to ask the venue management:

- What do the technicians expect from you in terms of lighting plans? When do they need these?
- What is the standard lighting setup for the theatre? If this is not adequate for your show, is there enough spare equipment to provide extra or special lighting effects? Are there any additional charges for rigging extra or special lighting? Are bulbs and spare equipment readily available and easy to find should something fail during the performances?
- When do you need to provide a script marked with lighting cues?
- How many rehearsals do the technicians normally attend?
- What happens if the technician falls ill or is otherwise unexpectedly unavailable for a show or rehearsal?

If the venue provides adequate equipment but no manpower at any price, you will have to take some responsibility for understanding the setup. No matter how much expertise you already have, or how little you actually may care about the lighting for this particular show, become familiar with the controls, location of the lamps and the fuse box, and how to obtain and fit spare bulbs. For rented venues, find out the procedure for calling in an electrician if there is a major problem with the lights. At some point, you may find this knowledge extremely useful.

If your venue does not automatically provide a technician to run lighting during dress rehearsals and performances, you will need to train someone to operate the lights during the technical run-through, dress rehearsals, and performances. You may also need someone to rig or at least fine-tune the lighting before the technical run-through takes place. Hopefully someone in the cast will volunteer a knowledgeable parent to help rig the lights or an older sibling to run the lights during the show. See the section, "Recruiting Extra Help" in chapter 14.

The following paragraphs discuss examples of lighting typically found in performance venues.

Overhead fluorescent lights only

These are common in a school hall or auditorium that doubles as the cafeteria, particularly if it is newly built and as yet without funding for stage lighting equipment. If you are not in a position to augment the available lighting through purchasing, renting, or borrowing, you will need to survey what you do have and work with it as best you can.

First, check to see if you can isolate the lights that are above the acting space. This will allow the audience to remain in darkness once the show begins while you can switch the lights above the acting area on and off between scenes as required. (See figure 15) Take care that the actors' faces are not in too much shadow if only the overhead lights on the stage area are used.

If you cannot isolate the lights for the stage or acting area — a common problem because of the way some rooms are wired — you may have to leave the lights on during the entire show. You may be able to use a total blackout occasionally, keeping in mind that audiences get nervous if a blackout lasts longer than a few seconds. Many school halls have windows that are hard to block completely, so if you are performing during the day, you will still have some light even if the lights are out.

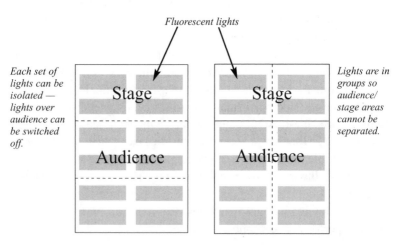

Figure 15 – Typical setups for fluorescent lighting

In this case, review if any lighting effects are an important part of the plot. Is a sudden blackout pivotal to the action? You may need to coach your actors how to act as if they cannot see in the "blackout." Plan how you will begin and end scenes and carry out stage scenery changes. If a scene begins by actors entering an empty stage or if it ends by actors exiting, leaving an empty stage behind, things are simple. Make sure your actors emphasize lines such as "It's dark in here" or "Aren't these club lights dazzling?" and carry out appropriate actions and stage business. This will give clues to lighting and atmosphere and help the audience establish location and mood.

In contrast, if the scene ends in a tableau of twenty people and the stage directions state "blackout," you will need to employ other methods of transition. One option is to draw the curtains, but you may have no curtains. Anyway, constant curtain opening and closing becomes slow and tedious. See if the scene is written so that the actors can exit naturally after their lines end. Another option is to have the actors freeze very definitively into position at the end of the scene. This can actually add to the drama and tension of the scene. Usually the audience will respond with applause, at which point the actors can break from position and exit or take the correct position for the following scene. Should the audience not applaud, direct the actors to remain in position for two to five seconds and then move off-stage.

Similarly, for scenes that begin with actors already on-stage, see if the action would work with the actors saying their opening lines as they come on-stage. Alternatively, they can take their positions, freeze, and then begin.

Scenery changes for constantly lit stages do not differ much from those with stage lighting. However, you may want to rehearse the changes a bit more thoroughly so they are precise and smooth. Exhort people not to *rush* the changes, but go through them at a steady pace. Someone tripping over the sofa in full view during a scene change is one showstopper you would probably prefer to skip. See the section, "Planning and Rehearsing Scene Changes," in chapter 14.

Standard stage lighting setup

Assuming you have either a proscenium or thrust stage or other area set aside for the action to take place, a typical stage lighting arrangement illuminates the front and sides of the actors. Lights should also be focused on areas upstage of the actors so they do not create silhouettes against the back curtain, although in some instances you may want to use this as an effect.

Normally, a set of Fresnels will supply general lighting while Lekos supply more sharp-edged, focused lighting. The lights are normally then wired to a control panel, where you can bring up or fade out different banks of lights, or even single lights.

A series of bars usually hangs across the top of the stage; lights are then hung from these. In addition, a bar is hung above the first few rows of the audience (or two bars are anchored vertically along the auditorium wall on either side), to provide a position for lights to illuminate the downstage area and apron of the stage.

Test the lights to check for any missing lenses or bulbs and to make sure they are all wired into the control panel. Obviously, there must be enough electricity, sockets, and cables available to have everything work properly at the same time. You and your lighting technician need to become familiar with using the controls. See figure 16.

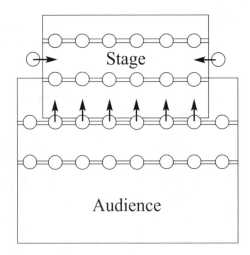

Figure 16 – Typical proscenium or thrust stage lighting
(Arrows indicate the direction the lights are pointing.)

Moveable spotlights

Moveable spotlights can effectively isolate and follow a single actor, particularly during a song or soliloquy. They do take rehearsal and practice so any movement is smooth and not shaky. Spotlights can also focus on small groups of actors.

Light lens accessories for special effects

Lights can quickly create a sense of place and atmosphere. One way is through the use of color: pinks and reds help establish a cheesy night-club mood in *Bugsy Malone*; pale cool blues establish the unfriendly, cold atmosphere of the orphanage bedroom in Annie; greens can create a ghastly effect in the underworld inhabited by the Phantom in the *Phantom of the Op'ry.*

Impressive effects can also be created through the use of *gobos*. These thin, square sheets of metal have patterns cut into them, which are then placed over a light. The light is then focused on the floor and backdrop to create an effect. For example, leaf patterns create forests in *Into the Woods;* vertical lines create a jail cell in *Joseph and the Amazing Technicolor Dreamcoat;* a star and moon pattern creates nighttime scenes of either romance or prayer meetings in *Guys and Dolls.*

Augmenting available lighting

Once you have surveyed your available lighting equipment, you need to decide if it provides adequate lighting for the show. Before you decide you absolutely require additional equipment, make sure you actually do.

If you do decide you need additional lighting, check that the venue can actually provide enough electricity and sockets to support extra spotlights or banks of lights without blowing the circuits. If necessary, have a qualified electrician measure the actual capacity of the circuits that will be used for lighting. Once you are convinced that your venue has the capacity for extra lighting, you can start to obtain it. Here are some options:

Purchasing

If you have a long-term commitment to the group and the budget, owning your own equipment can provide flexibility and save you money over time, assuming you care for it properly and have a secure place to store it when it's not in use. Check that your insurance will cover accidental damage or theft.

Borrowing

Schools and amateur groups will often let you borrow equipment. Sometimes parents may have some equipment or have access to equipment. Here you do need to be sure your insurance or the lender's will cover any problems. If not, you need to consider the risk factor of having to replace equipment if it's stolen or damaged. Also, check that the equipment will be complete and available when you need it; there's nothing like being told the guy with the key is now away for three weeks when you turn up at Scout Center with the van and three parents to collect the equipment.

Renting

Technical lighting companies have a wide range of equipment available — at a price, but you do not need to worry about long-term storage and maintenance. Again, check that any damage or theft is covered either by your venue insurance or through the rental company.

Considerations in coaching actors under stage lighting

If you are using stage lighting, it may not light the entire stage properly. Test this. Ask one of your performers to move around the stage, particularly to the apron area. See if they are ever in shadow. Try to adjust the lights so all areas are clearly lit.

If you cannot change the lighting, watch out for actors who move into shadow during their scenes. This frequently happens when they move downstage. Other times, performers will react to the discomfort of bright lights in their faces by moving out of their range. Coach these performers to stay in a position where they can feel the light on their faces, and not go too far downstage.

Sound Effects

In addition to the music, singing, and dialog, the script may call for particular sound effects. These signal important action within the story and can often contribute to the energy, mood, and tempo of the show: telephones ring, doorbells chime, gunshots are fired, screams echo.

Check the script for sound effects; in addition to looking at any publishers notes, re-read the script so nothing is left out. Make a list of the effects required. Then plan how to produce them. As usual, check with your venue to find out what might be available for sound effects.

Live sound effects

Sound effects fall into two categories, live and recorded. Live sound effects are produced off-stage during the production. Whoever is responsible for producing them needs to follow the script closely and produce the sounds exactly on cue, even if some lines have been missed or said out of order. The person on the prompt book can often double as the sound effects person if there are not too many effects. Common examples of live sound effects include the following:

- Knocking at the door
- Isolated screams
- Bicycle bell
- Microwave bell (bicycle bell works well here)
- Door buzzer (mounted on a piece of wood)
- Teacher's bell ringing
- Blanks in a gun
- Ghoulish laughter

Recorded sounds

Numerous sound effects have now been collected on CDs and tapes and are widely available. They are perfect when the sound is otherwise impractical to produce live; for example, car brakes squealing or a motorcycle crashing. You can also download individual sound effects from the Internet or buy entire collections from the publisher. Unlike tapes, CDs provide the flexibility of cuing up to an exact place. You need to arrange for a CD player and speakers loud enough for the size of your performance hall. Ideally, your speakers should be only where the sound is supposedly coming from. Common recorded sound effects include the following:

- Chandelier crashing to the floor
- Glass window breaking
- Police sirens
- Thunder and stormy weather
- Birds chirping
- Traffic noises
- Church bells
- Waves on a beach

Integrating sound effects into the show

Try to start using sound effects as soon as you start running through scenes and acts. Early use of sound effects will make them seem more natural to the actors, who will be less likely to be startled or amused by the effects. If possible, run through that section of dialog several times, concentrating on the sound effect. In this way, you can adjust volume levels of recorded sounds as required and the operator in charge of live sounds can practice producing them exactly on cue. The absolute latest point at which to introduce sound is the technical rehearsal, which is already a busy time.

Sound (Amplification) Equipment

Sound equipment for voice projection

Your participants attend your workshops to learn how to project their voices, so microphones are not essential, especially for spoken dialog or chorus numbers. On the other hand, microphones can be useful luxuries for solo and duet singing scenes. Microphones help the actors project their voices above the musical accompaniment. Because they do not need to force or strain their voices, they can concentrate more fully on the melody, meaning, and mood of the song. Also, if the leading character sings several lines, and then a chorus of thirty weighs in with the refrain, the single voice will seem overwhelmed. This problem is solved when a soloist uses a microphone.

Assessing sound equipment at the performance venue

Check to see what sound equipment your venue provides, and see if the rental fee includes the services of a technician. You may be able to hire a technician for an hourly rate; some contracts insist you use only technicians provided by the venue, even though you will need to pay extra for their services. This rule generally ensures the technician understands how to use the equipment. You may also be able to rent equipment at additional cost. Review the fine print of any rental or hire contract — what if the equipment malfunctions? Will a speedy replacement be provided at no additional charge?

If you decide you need additional or different sound equipment than that provided at the venue, determine what equipment is most suitable and determine its costs. Whatever equipment you choose to use, aim to set up the equipment and test for feedback levels long before the audience starts filling the performance hall, ideally before the first technical rehearsal.

Choices in microphones

If your venue does not provide microphones (either as part of the rental or at additional cost) you can, as with the other stage equipment, buy, rent, or borrow microphones. A range of sophisticated mikes can be rented from theatrical sound and lighting agencies.

Cordless microphones

Cordless mikes come in different varieties. Tiny radio mikes are expensive, but they are also nearly invisible and provide maximum flexibility. The microphone itself is miniscule and can be clipped to a collar or lapel. Larger, hand-held cordless microphones are less costly and still offer the advantage of not having cords to trip over. If you use cordless microphones, stock up on spare batteries of the correct size so you don't run out of batteries mid-show.

Wired microphones

Microphones can be hooked up via wires to a guitar (or other) amplifier and then wired to speakers, or they can be hooked up to a combined amplifier/speaker. Speakers need to be adequate for the size for your performance hall. Depending on the quality of the wired microphones, amplifier, and speakers, you can obtain a full, round sound at much less expense than with wireless microphones. Usually the wire will be fairly long, which allows range of movement, although the primary use of microphones tends to be for romantic songs, where the singers usually stay in one spot.

Alternatively, you can buy or borrow a cheap "boogie," or boom box, or a karaoke kit, which consists of two microphones whose connecting wires run through a combination amplifier and speaker. The quality is usually not as good as with separate mikes, amplifier, and speakers. The wires between the mikes and the "box" are usually fairly short. Before you decide to buy, check the size of the stage in comparison to the length of the wires and decide if your actors will still have enough freedom of movement for their musical numbers. Despite the limitations of this arrangement, the output from this setup is perfectly adequate for many shows and performance halls, and the cost is minimal. With either type of wired microphones, check that wires are placed so that no one can trip over them.

175

Setting up microphones for rehearsal and performance

For most performances of most shows, you can manage with just two microphones. Set up "home" stations for each one. The "home" might be a low microphone stand for hand-held mikes or a box for radio mikes, usually at the center downstage edge of the stage.

It is very helpful to color-code each microphone and its "home." It is best to use colors that are easily distinguished in low lighting conditions, or to use a color and a symbol, such as an orange square or a white circle.

To avoid feedback, any loudspeakers need to be farther downstage, or off the stage, than the performers will move. If performers using microphones are on the same "plane" as the loudspeakers, feedback occurs.

Rehearsing with microphones

The use of microphones, or mikes, during performances needs to be choreographed as much as the big dance numbers. Luckily, it seldom takes as long. Rehearse with your performers so they know exactly what they need to do with the mikes when they are finished with them. Normally they have one of three options: 1) hand their mikes on to another actor, who will use the mike immediately, 2) hand it to a member of the stage crew, or 3) return it to its "home."

The actors need to have a chance to practice with the mikes. They need time to learn how to do the following:

- Adjust their voice volume to prevent feedback while still being loud enough to be heard.
- Keep the mikes the right distance consistently from their mouths so their voices don't fade in and out. (The first "talkie" number in *Singing in the Rain* illustrates this phenomenon perfectly, and so, most likely, will your performers.)
- Turn the mikes on and off.
- Avoid becoming tangled up in the wires, if using wired mikes. This applies to both performers and stage crew.

If you are renting mikes, you may not be picking them up until the technical rehearsal, so plan for the group to practice with the mikes at the beginning of that session. Once mikes arrive, everyone will want to use them, so you may as well give them a chance. If you have mikes available earlier, schedule a short "microphone class" so everyone can learn how to use them properly.

Knowing how to use a microphone helps build the confidence of a performer, even if they don't use them in this particular show. And you never know when someone may need to take over a part, and having experience with the microphones will make the transition easier. Finally, using a microphone is a skill that your players will, at some point, be grateful to you for teaching. How many of us have arrived to give a short presentation and then been handed a microphone, experienced the screech of feedback, and vowed never to set foot near a podium again?

Teaching your group to use a microphone

Here are some suggested steps in teaching your group how to use a microphone.

First, gather the group around you and show them the equipment. Demonstrate how various parts fit together and what each component does. Explain where the microphones and their "homes" will be during the show. Explain the power sources (battery or mains electricity — the type accessed through wall outlets) and where they are.

Liver Lips Louis confidently uses a microphone during a solo in Guys and Dolls.

Once you have explained the basics and the jargon, ask the group to form two lines on the stage. They then can handle the microphones and practice typical maneuvers. Be sure to do the following:

1. If using radio mikes, show how the mikes clip on to lapels, collars, or shirtfronts and how to make sure they point in the right direction. Have the members of each line clip on the microphone, turn it on, speak or sing, take it off, and pass it to the next person. Often there is very little time to put on the microphone.

2. If using hand-held mikes, show the group how to turn it on and off, at what angle the microphone should be held, and how far away from the mouth they should hold it. Hand the mike to the first person in each line, ask them to turn it on,

177

hold it properly, speak or sing into it, turn it off, and pass it to the next person.

3. If you are using microphones with wires, demonstrate how easy it is to become tangled up in and trip on the wire. Then ask them to practice picking up the microphone, switching it on, speaking or singing into it, returning it to its home, and handing it to another actor.

4. Show them how the distance between the microphone and the amplifier/speakers affects feedback. Have each person speak some lines while wandering too close and experience what happens.

5. Explain and demonstrate that using a microphone is not a cue to start whispering. Have them try whispering and then using a normal speaking voice.

6. Set the mikes in a stand. Have each performer come up to the microphone and sing a couple of lines from one of their songs. Do they need to adjust their singing volume because of the microphone?

7. Again using microphones in a stand, have each performer experiment with moving their mouths closer and then farther away from the mike while singing. Are any effects created they would like to try during the show? Are there any effects you would like them to avoid?

Equipment for Live or Recorded Musical Accompaniment

It's hard work putting on an a cappella musical. You have a choice of using live accompaniment or a pre-recorded accompaniment CD or tape. Both require equipment or instruments and both present their own advantages and challenges.

Live music accompaniment

You may need both instruments and amplification equipment for live music.

Piano

Unlike most musical instruments, the pianist does not usually bring along the piano. So check with your venue and ask some essential questions: 1) Is there a piano? 2) Do all the keys work? 3) Will it be available at the performance hall at the times of the final music rehearsals, dress rehearsals, and performances? 4) Is it in tune? If not, are you willing to pay to have it tuned? There is nothing like having to track down and arrange delivery of a tuned piano the morning of the first performance to raise whatever levels of excitement and stress you may be already experiencing.

Electronic keyboard and other instruments

If you plan to use a keyboard or any other electronic instruments, such as a guitar, check if your musicians will provide them. These instruments need an amplifier and speakers appropriate for the size of the hall. You may need to rent or borrow the instruments and/or the amplifier and speakers.

Check where your power source is in relationship to the keyboard — you may need to use extension cables. If the cables are where your cast or audience may be walking, you need to cover them with materials that meet any health and safety standards.

Recorded accompaniment

If you are performing to music that will be played on a CD or tape, check if the venue provides a sound system that you can play it over. Alternatively, you will need an appropriate stereo player with speakers substantial enough for the size of your performance venue.

As with other electronic equipment, check where your power source is in relationship to the stereo player — you may need to use extension cables. If the cables must be laid where your cast or audience may be walking, you need to cover them with materials that meet any health and safety standards.

Chapter 13

Building an Audience for Your Show

Publicity and Promotion

There is almost no end to the promotional activities you can undertake to publicize your show. However, your best audience is the families and friends of your performers, so it is important that you help your group members promote the show to them.

As rehearsals progress, spend a few minutes talking about how much people enjoy coming to a show where they know a cast member. Ask them to think about who might like to come — friends, relatives, neighbors, or members of their soccer team, scout group, or church. Also, remind them what an interesting and exciting script they are presenting and what a good "night out" it will be. Mention a few of the more exciting scenes with comments such as "I can't wait until everyone sees the pillow fight," or "The car race will be a real hit with everyone who comes."

Announce the cost of tickets — which may seem high if you are planning to rent elaborate costumes or a venue with top-class facilities — and explain that the show is well worth the expense. Some of your potential audience may have an unrealistic idea of how much it costs to put on a show and expect a show with kids to be inexpensive. By mentioning the ticket prices up front, you avoid "sticker shock" later on.

Website

If your group is an ongoing workshop, you may already have a website. If so, put information about the show on the site as soon as possible.

Flyers

At least six weeks before the show, you need to give your performers some simple flyers that can be posted on notice boards or distributed to friends and family. The flyers do not have to be elaborate or large. Black and white photocopies of hand-printed information are adequate. A half-letter size sheet (U.S.) or A5 sheet (U.K.) provides enough room for all the necessary information. Computer-printed flyers can include all sorts of pictures and typefaces if you have the time to set them up. If you do use a computer printer, make sure it produces a *waterproof* copy. If you are trying to save on costs, provide a single flyer to each cast member — they are often willing to photocopy it themselves.

The flyer should clearly state the name of the show, dates and days of week of the show, start time and approximate finish time, location and cost for children/adult/student/senior citizen tickets if you are using tiered pricing. Directions and a map to the venue are very useful additions. If the play is not widely known, some information about the story and its appropriateness for different age groups is helpful to parents who have to decide which members of the family would enjoy the show. If your group already has a website with information about the musical, be sure to include the website address. Your group members can post these flyers on their school or church boards. They can also hand them out to their friends — whose parents will find clear information a godsend.

Local newspapers

If you have a small community paper or a local paper with an arts section, the editor may be interested in printing a short press release and, very importantly, pictures. Look at the local papers and see if they seem to run stories about amateur theatre groups. Check, too, whether such publicized groups consistently seem to be running advertising in the same edition. If you are on a tight budget, you may not wish to spend money on advertising, and it may be impossible to get the story printed without it.

Finally, you may have some parents who are already working in media or marketing and who might be interested in helping publicize your show.

Informing the audience of a different performance venue

If you have planned to have the performance in a different venue than your rehearsals from the beginning, announce it to your group as soon as possible and keep reminding them. Point out the advantages of the change — usually these boil down to having better facilities for performance. If possible, list the performance venue on the general workshop information flyer and on your website about your group.

If you must change the performance venue for reasons beyond your control, such as the owner has decided to sell the property or the venue was double-booked, inform the group and parents as soon as possible. Again, try to cite positive reasons for the change.

Tickets

Producing tickets

You may be renting a venue that provides full ticketing and seat reservation services. However, most amateur groups must produce and sell their own tickets. Arrange for tickets to be printed and available for sale no later than four weeks before the show opens.

You will need a set of tickets for each separate performance date and time. So if you are doing three evening performances on Thursday, Friday, and Saturday and a matinee on Saturday, you will need four sets of tickets. We recommend that you produce each set on different colored paper or cardstock. To determine how many tickets you need to produce in each set, simply count up the available seats at the venue.

If you are on a tight budget, you — or a child or parent volunteer with an artistic bent — can design the tickets on a word processor, using the table feature. Whether you want to include some sort of design or picture on the ticket is up to you. However, do make sure the tickets have all the essential information, including the name of your group, name of the show, venue, full venue address including the zip code or postcode, day of week, date, time, and cost.

The day of the week helps clarify exactly which date the theatergoer is coming. We recommend you include the complete venue address, even if it is the local school or at the same venue you used for rehearsals. You cannot assume that everyone knows where "St. Michael's Church, West Oaks" actually is. Some people will not look at the ticket until they set off for the show, may be running late, and then will want to know exactly where it is located. See figure 17 for a sample ticket.

To further simplify production, all tickets should display the cost of all varieties of tickets you may be expected to sell; for example, adult, child, student, senior citizens, and so forth. You may wish to clarify your definition of "child;" for example, is a child someone under twelve? sixteen? eighteen? When you sell the ticket, simply circle the price that applies. At performances, your ticket collectors can check that the ticket holder seems to fit the description.

From the word processor, you can print these out onto thin cardstock, and cut out individual tickets. If you are using letter-size paper (U.S.), you can usually produce eight small tickets per page (portrait) or six large tickets per page (landscape). If you are using A4 paper (U.K.), you can produce eight small tickets per page (portrait) or six large tickets per page (landscape).

If you are using a computer printer, make sure the ink is *waterproof.* You can also take your master sheet to be photocopied onto thin cardstock.

Cardstock can usually be found at office supply stores. Take care that it is not too thick, or it will not feed through a printer or photocopier. You may be obliged to buy many more sheets than you will need for this performance; you can always put any spare sheets aside to use with your next show. To calculate the minimum number of sheets of cardstock of each color you will need, divide the total number of seats to be sold by the number of tickets per sheet you will be printing. That number, plus some extra in case of errors, will give you the number of sheets of cardstock you will need of each color. For example, 100 tickets divided by 8 = 12.5, so you will need about 15 sheets.

Alternatively, if you have the money and have found a supplier, you can get tickets professionally printed.

You also need to decide whether you are going to offer reserved seating. This is almost impossible to do in a venue where you must put out folding chairs for each performance. The seats will not be numbered, and if nothing else, it would be difficult to set them out in the exact same configuration each evening. In this type of seating arrangement, tell your group to remind their audience that the seating is "first come — first serve." You, of course, can reserve seats by taping signs on them. Whether you will allow your cast to do the same is up to you — it can result in a bit of a free-for-all when the cast first arrives to do the show.

If the venue does have fixed, numbered seats, you can offer reserved seats. Number the tickets in a system that follows the venues seating plan; for example A1, A2, A3, B1, B2, B3. If you know how, you can even do a mail merge with your word processor and number the tickets automatically. Once the tickets are produced, try to keep each set in order. Produce a copy of the seating plan for each evening and clearly label it with the day and date of the performance. You can then show the seating plan to the ticket-buyers, who then choose a seat. Carefully mark out the seats chosen (in pencil, in case of a sudden change in seat selection) and hand the correct tickets to the buyer.

Even if you do not use reserved seating, you will find it helpful to number your tickets, starting with one and continuing to the number of seats available in the hall. Assuming you keep them in order, you can see at glance how many you have sold. Numbered tickets also help you keep the tally of ticket sales if you have a ticket sale competition (see next section).

Figure 17 – Sample ticket

Selling tickets

It is vital to start selling the tickets a reasonable time before the performances. Starting four weeks before the show, make tickets available for sale before and after each rehearsal. If you have distributed your promotional flyers two weeks prior, you should start seeing kids come in with ticket money by this time. A ticket sale competition also helps. Keep reminding the group that you are expecting sell-out crowds and that they should encourage their friends and family to buy their tickets as early as possible.

Do not distribute tickets to the kids to sell, and in general, never give out tickets without first receiving payment. Don't hold tickets at the door without payment. You and your group have spent much time and effort putting together an excellent evening of entertainment, and your audience can either pay in advance or pay at the door.

In a workshop situation, you need to recruit some parents to act as "ticket secretaries." Before and after rehearsals, and for about thirty minutes before each performance, the ticket secretary oversees the cashbox, collects money, records information for the ticket sale competition if you are running one, and hands out tickets. You can use a different person each time you need a ticket secretary, as long as you are willing to explain what they have to do each time. If you are working with a secondary school class or drama club, you may be able to secure the help of a responsible student, or the club treasurer, to act as ticket secretary. (See the section, "Recruiting Extra Help" in chapter 14.)

To make ticket sales easier, especially if different people are helping at each rehearsal and performance, organize a cashbox big enough to hold unsold tickets, seating plans if you are using reserved seating, ticket sales record sheets if you are running a competition, and pens and pencils. The cashbox also needs a float for giving change. Make sure the cashbox is never left unattended and that your helper hands it over to you after ticket sales are complete for that day.

Ticket sale competitions

To encourage sales, we have found it effective and fun to run a cast competition: Who can sell the most tickets? A prize — usually a big box of chocolates or other candy — is awarded at the end of the workshop season or on the last night. If you run a ticket competition, your ticket secretaries must record how many tickets each child sells. Keep a record sheet in the cash box to track this information.

At rehearsals, post a tally chart, showing cast names and the number of tickets they've sold so far. Update it each week. This generates interest and reminds everyone to sell tickets. When you update your tally chart, mark the record sheet so no sold tickets are counted twice.

Decide when you want the competition to end. Usually it is easiest if you limit the competition to pre-show ticket sales. This helps to get more cash in earlier. As an additional contest, you can also run a tickets-at-the door competition, which requires some last-minute tallying. When selling tickets at the door, the ticket secretary must ask the audience member to name the cast member who persuaded them to come to the show and keep an accurate record of this information. You can announce the winner of the tickets-at-the door contest at your final workshop or during intermission at the last performance.

Programs

Your audience will expect a program when they come to the show. This can be an elaborate affair, filled with sponsorship advertisers, photos, and background information. Or you can opt for a simple photocopied or printed single sheet of paper folded in half.

Check with your licensing arrangements about how the title of the show is to be presented on the front cover or title page of your program. You need to include the authors' names and possibly, if the show was based on a novel or stage play, the name of the original author. You may also need to include the name of the publisher, with words, such as "produced by arrangement with Contemporary Drama Service."

Check your master cast list carefully and take care to include every single cast member's name and every role they play. Here you can list any extra backstage helpers as well as the musical director, musicians, choreographer, and anyone else with a named role. Before you print copies of the program, invite the cast and anyone else available to proof the spelling of their names. People get upset if their names are incorrect on the program.

A program is an excellent place to express your gratitude to all those who have contributed skills, time, properties, or other items to make the show a success. Be careful about mentioning too many specific names. You are bound to miss someone, who will then feel slighted. Be sure to thank the cast and their parents, in general terms, for all their hard work and support. (See figures 18 and 19 for an example of the pages of a simple program.)

Blank

or thank you's to parents,
cast and others
if not enough room inside

and/or
information about your group
or the next show.

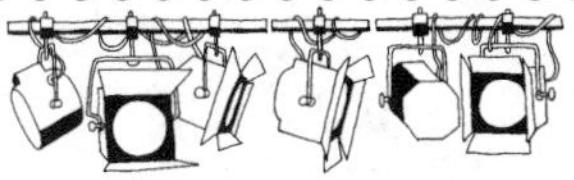

The Actors of
Adele Lawson's
School of Theatre
proudly present

Guys and Dolls

by Frank Lesser and Abe Burrows
Produced by Josef Weinberger Ltd.
in arrangement with publisher.

The Imaginary Theatre
May 20, 21, and 22, 2005

Figure 18 – Simple program front and back covers

Production Team

Director	Adele Lawson
Musical director	Lyn Mackenzie
Drummer	Robin Cowat
Props/Set	Terry Lawton
Backcloth	Howarth Wrightson Ltd.
Lighting	Duncan Armstrong
Hot Box Costumes	Linda Cameron
Mission Band Costumes	Sale Grammar School
Other costumes	Parents
Tickets	Lynne Woods
Prompt	Edna Lawson
Stage Crew	Lynne Woods
	Thomas Chapman
	Adam Chapman
	Poppy Wainwright
Callboys	Bea Chapman
	Jane Wainwright

A note from the director

Congratulations once again to all the cast on another excellent performance — they go from strength to strength! In particular, you will notice the development of some very strong singing voices. From a personal point of view, I am always impressed by the self-discipline and concentration the children show in rehearsals. They are a delight to work with.

A big Thank You as always to everyone — parents, friends, brothers, and sisters — who has helped in so many ways with this production. I couldn't do it without such help and talent.

Special thanks to Terry Lawton who has amazed us all with some fabulous props and to Linda Cameron for sewing the gorgeous Hot Box costumes.

Adele

The Cast

Sky Masterson	Kayleigh Hill
Sarah Brown	Julie Duane
Nathan Detroit	Lesley-Anne Carter
Miss Adelaide	Elizabeth Lawton
Nicely-Nicely Johnson	Lindsey Flanagan
Benny Southstreet	Thomas Campbell
Harry the Horse	David Brow
Big Jule	Owyn Rowland
Liver Lips Louis/Mimi	Jemma Lochrie
Rusty Charlie/Dancer	Helen Smiddy
Scranton Slim	Poppy Wainwritht
Society Max	Ellis Wainwright
Angie the Ox/Missionary	Laura Dixon
Lt. Brannigan/Dancer	Kirsty Newton
Arvide Abernathy	Emily Jones
General Cartwright	Clare Whitlow
Mission Band	Gemma Dixon
	Janine Cross
	Rebecca Addison
Hot Box Dancers	Jodie Green
	Chloe Ford
	Jodie Leach
Guys	Thomas Chapman
	Thomas Hurdsfield
	Christopher Murray
	Kristina Coyne
	Katie Swift
	Christina Garrett
Dolls	Molly Chapman
	Laura Moran
	Melissa Coyne
	Eleanor Smith

Figure 19 – Simple program, inside pages

Chapter 14

Putting It All Together -
the Final Rehearsals

During these rehearsals, which start around session 30, you are still in the "polishing" stage, but are now running entire acts without stopping. At this point, start to finalize the movement, management, and use of scenery and properties on-stage and backstage. During the technical and dress rehearsals (usually the last three), you also put in lighting and sound effects, add all costumes and any makeup, and integrate any live accompaniment into the show. See the sample 36-week rehearsal schedule in chapter 3 for more details.

Recruiting Extra Help for the Final Rehearsals and Performances

Although your cast members will be handling set changes, non-cast members, mostly parents, now need to be recruited in earnest to help backstage as prompt, callboy, lighting and sound assistants, and dressing room/greenroom monitors. You also need people to act as ticket secretaries for before and after rehearsals and before performances, ticket collectors, ushers, refreshment salespeople, chair stackers, and end-of-performance set dismantlers. The roles of these helpers are described in detail in the following paragraphs. Remember, as the director, you must not formally take *any* backstage role. You will have enough to do to keep everything together.

About two months before the show opens, send a letter stating exactly what roles you need help with in putting on the show. Explain in the letter that a sign up sheet or rota will be posted in the rehearsal hall, and you really, really need it to be filled in. If you have been mentioning this all along in letters home and ongoing

189

conversations with parents, your request should come as no surprise, and you may have already filled some of the roles. Examples of these letters and a roster sheet are shown in figures 20 and 21. See the sample 36-week rehearsal schedule in chapter 3 for more details about the timing and content of these letters.

The roles of your helpers are as follows:

Backstage

Callboy – The callboy needs to attend a couple of rehearsals before the technical rehearsal so he or she can watch and listen to the action and learn when a scene is about to finish. The callboy then needs to be available for all dress rehearsals and performances, so this is a big role. The callboy has the important responsibility of making sure the actors for each scene are ready to go on-stage. If your group has been following the rehearsal methods outlined in this book, they will have a fairly clear idea how long the scenes are and how much time they have for costumes changes, but you still need someone who will consistently round up everyone and see they are ready to go on-stage. This person can also help to quiet the kids down as they come off-stage.

Prompt – This is another critical and time-intensive role. The prompt needs to start attending a few rehearsals before the technical rehearsal, then come to all the dress rehearsals and performances. The prompt holds a "prompt book," which is the complete, final script. The prompt simply follows along in the script with the action on the stage, and if an actor forgets a line or "dries," the prompt "prompts" the actor, that is, calls out the first few words of the line so that the actor can carry on. For more details on the prompt's role, see the section, "Using a prompt" in chapter 9.

Lighting assistant – The lighting assistant needs to attend all rehearsals and performances beginning with the technical rehearsal. He or she should get a marked script before the technical rehearsal and meet with you to go over lighting cues. The lighting assistant checks that the lights are rigged properly before each dress rehearsal and show, and then runs the lights from the control board.

Sound assistant – The sound assistant needs to attend all rehearsals and performances beginning with the technical rehearsal. He or she should get a marked script before the technical rehearsal, and meet with you to go over sound cues. The sound assistant

Adele Lawson's School of Theatre
23 Any Street, Townsville 54321
Tel: 111-222-3333 – Cell/mobile: 444-555-6666

April 14, 2005

Dear Parents,

For anyone who has not paid today, fees will be due for this half term (6 sessions, April 18 – May 30) as soon as possible, preferably next week.

$42.00 (checks to A. Firth)

In the meantime, rehearsals are continuing and excitement is brewing among the cast as production week approaches. We have also had some great scenery building workshops, and the set is just about complete, thanks to some very committed and talented parents.

A reminder of rehearsal/performance dates: PLEASE NOTE STARTING MAY 15 WE WILL BE WORKING IN THE PERFORMANCE VENUE. Map and other details provided two weeks before.

Tech/Dress Rehearsal	NE Theatre	Sat., May 15	2–5P.M.	Full Costume
Tech/Dress Rehearsal	NE Theatre	Sun., May 16	2–5P.M.	Full Costume
Dress Rehearsal	NE Theatre	Wed., May 19	6–9:30P.M.	Full Costume
Performance	NE Theatre	Thurs., May 20	7:30–9:30P.M.	Full Costume
Performance	NE Theatre	Fri., May 21	7:30–9:30P.M.	Full Costume
Performance	NE Theatre	Sat., May 22	7:30–9:30P.M.	Full Costume

Tickets will be on sale at every rehearsal from now on. <u>If any parents can help with distributing them at 1:45 P.M. or 4 P.M. on rehearsal days, this would be most appreciated.</u> Seats could sell out quickly judging by past productions, so buy early. Adults $8, children $4. There will be a prize for the person/family selling the most tickets. In order to ensure good audiences, everyone in the cast needs to aim to sell at least 10 tickets.

By now, you should have received a list of <u>costume requirements</u>. The children can start bringing them to the rehearsals, as long as they bring them home at the end of each session. If you are uncertain whether a costume will work, please show it to me at the <u>end</u> of a session. Do label all items with the child's name.

We will need lots of Parent Power for the show. If each family could provide one adult to help either backstage or in the front of the house on one of the dates above, we should be covered. If you could complete the slip below and return it, or sign up on the roster at the rehearsal hall, I would be most grateful. In particular, I could do with some strong bodies on the last night to dismantle the set, load the van, etc. I am thrilled to announce parents have already volunteered for the "Big 5" of lights, sound, prompt, callboy, and makeup.

The last workshop of the season will be May 29. Some group members would like this to be a cast party with food. We are exploring this idea. Many thanks, and I look forward to seeing you!

Adele

Name _____ Phone number_____

Child's name _____

I am available to help for _____ (total number of nights) on any or only of the following date(s):

May 17____   May 19____   May 20____   May 21____

May 22 (during show)____   May 22 (at end of show)____

Figure 20 – Sample letter asking for help backstage

Parent Power — Please sign up.

Besides the "Big 5" (Prompt, Lights, Sound, Callboy, and Makeup), if every family could provide one adult helper we will be covered. As you can see, we really need some more help with backstage monitors and refreshment sellers. Please see me if interested. Please note actual performances are anticiptated to run 7:30 – 9:30 P.M. The times listed below are when your help is needed!

Role	No. of nights needed.	Dress Rehearsal May 19 (6–9:30 P.M.)	Performance May 20 (7–10 P.M.)	Performance May 21 (7–10 P.M.)	During performance May 22 (7–10 P.M.)	After performance May 22 (9:30–11P.M.)
Callboy	6	Joyce ◄———————————————►				
Lights	5	Ruth ◄———————————————►				
Prompt	6	Peter ◄———————————————►				
Sound	5	Sean ◄———————————————►				
Makeup	4	Wendy ◄———————————————►				
Backstage monitors (2 per night)	1	1._____ 2._____	1._____ 2._____	1._____ 2._____	1._____ 2._____	
Ticket Secretary before/after rehearsal	1	1.(B)_____ 2.(A)_____	1.(B)_____ 2.(A)_____			
Ticket Secretary/ takers (2 per show)	1		1._____ 2._____	1._____ 2._____	1._____ 2._____	
Refreshment sellers (3 each performance)	1		1._____ 2._____ 3._____	1._____ 2._____ 3._____	1._____ 2._____ 3._____	
Dismantle sets (as many as possible!)	1					1.George 2._____ 3._____

Figure 21 – Sample sign-up sheet (Roster)

checks that all sound equipment works and then runs all sound effects and recorded music. If you are using an accompaniment track, the musical director might run the music. If you have only a few sound effects, you may be able to get away with having the prompt or lighting assistant do the sound effects.

Makeup assistant – The makeup assistant needs to attend the makeup/dress rehearsal (usually, there is only one dress rehearsal with makeup) and the performances. If you have decided that the actors need makeup, you will need one or two adults willing to monitor its use and make sure the kids clean up afterward.

Greenroom/backstage monitors – Two or three adult volunteers need to be in the dressing rooms or waiting room for each of the final rehearsals and all of the performances. These adults can assist with any speedy costume changes, help keep general order, and be a point of reference should a real emergency, such as a fire or injury, arise. You can have different parents act as monitors each night. Since each adult helper only needs to help out one night, this is usually an easy role to fill.

Set dismantling/loading onto transport (if required) at end of the show – At the end of the show, you may need to dismantle the set either to dispose of it or to ship it back to the company you rented it from. Your best crew for this is usually a collection of dads, older brothers, and other strong helpers available immediately after the final performance.

Front of house – In addition to backstage helpers, you will need help to run the "Front of house." Front of house refers to activities that deal directly with audience members, such as selling tickets or ushering people to their seats.

Ticket secretary – The ticket secretary can be different for each rehearsal and performance, although you will need one for before and after each rehearsal, beginning four weeks before the show. The ticket secretary sells tickets, collects cash/checks, and records information for the ticket sales competition if you are running one. Once they have fulfilled their duties, they can then easily watch the show afterwards, so you should find ticket secretaries relatively easy to recruit. They will be handling cash, so you need to feel they are trustworthy. See the section, "Tickets" in chapter 13.

Ticket collector – Someone needs to collect tickets from the audience as they arrive. In most cases, the ticket secretary can perform this task.

Ushers – If you have reserved seating, you need ushers to take the audience members to their seats. This person can also hand out programs. Usually ushers are not necessary for open seating. You may find it easier, especially if you are expecting a full house, to simply leave the programs on the seats.

Refreshment sales – Refreshments are not strictly necessary, but your audience will enjoy the option of a snack before the show or during the intermission, especially if the show is long. You can also make some extra money this way.

Depending on what you want to sell, you may need two sets of people. Some will oversee the sales of pre-wrapped candy and canned drinks. Others need to be near facilities for hot water and will brew tea and coffee and provide extras like sugar, sweetener, and milk.

Helpers working the refreshment tables will need a float for making change. Put up signs that list what is for sale and the price of each item clearly. Make sure there are plenty of bins for cans and wrappers, and know where the mop is in case of spills. In hot weather, canned soft drinks need to be kept on ice in coolers.

If there are any rules against bringing in drinks or snacks to all or any part of the venue, make sure you follow them, even if this means no refreshments.

Chair setup at beginning/stacking at end/clearing up – In some venues, you will need to set up the chairs before the show and put them away after the show. You can usually get the cast to help you do this before the show, as they will have plenty of spare energy. You may need parental help at the end of the show, when you may also need to sweep the floor, clean the kitchen if used, and leave the venue as you found it.

Roles you do not need help with

Although you should certainly welcome adult help, and will need it, we have found it is usually not ideal to have adults act as stage crew or to take responsibility for all backstage tasks as the "Stage Manager." We strongly recommend that the cast act as stage crew; if coached and prepared, kids crave having the real responsibility of getting the scenes changed. If an adult suddenly shows up to "run things," you will lose the commitment of the kids.

For the adult, a stage management role requires committing a huge amount of time, and you already need to find people who can fulfill other time-intensive and truly critical roles such as the lighting and sound assistants, callboy, or prompt.

However, if you are staging a show that is technically complicated and you have a volunteer who is aware of the commitment required, you may feel more comfortable with an adult stage manager backstage. Make sure he or she is totally aware of any backstage responsibilities the kids have taken on, so there is no "take over" of backstage tasks already assigned to cast members. An adult stage manager helps by reminding the crew what they have to do next, rounding them up, and keeping them calm. The stage manager should try to avoid doing anything the stage crew can do for themselves, but he or she can step in if there is a true calamity, for example, scenery on wheels rolling off the stage into the orchestra pit.

Planning and Rehearsing Scene Changes

Preparing the cast to handle set changes

A "core" stage crew chosen from the cast, with occasional help from other cast members, can handle most scene changes during a performance. There are several advantages in using the cast for the stage crew. Getting the cast members involved in running the show increases their sense of ownership and responsibility for the entire show. If your scene changes take place in front of the audience, which they often do in musicals, you preserve the continuity and atmosphere by having the actors move the scenery; there's little mileage in introducing black-clad stage crew members into a play about orphans in the 1930s.

Having actors double as stage crew usually lessens the possibility of a crew member suddenly dropping out. Of course, actors drop out as well, but you can quickly draft in another actor to cover the stage duties — because you have established that actors do help backstage.

Although you may insist that all actors — even leads — are responsible for helping with scene changes and for bringing on props, you will need a core team. Ask for volunteers, focusing your spiel on chorus members whose costumes may already be dark-colored or non-descript and who do not have many split-second costume changes. In other words, in *Annie*, orphans, rather than the Boylan Sisters, have the more appropriate garb for scene changes. In *Bugsy Malone*, the gangsters have less attention-grabbing costumes than the molls. They are also less likely to be making last-minute adjustments to their makeup and hairstyles and more likely to be available when scene changes take place.

Use volunteers only, and don't draft just anyone into the team. You need people who are truly interested and committed. When seeking volunteers, you can, however, describe in all truthfulness the many appeals of the role: it is critical to the show's success, and it requires intelligence, concentration, physical prowess, and stealth.

Those performers who get restless in the dressing room often shine in the role of stage crew. They enjoy having something special to do and respond well to the extra responsibility, authority, and in many cases, audience exposure that being in the stage crew entails. As ever, most of the audience has come to see as much of their friends or children as possible. Having chorus members double as stage crew gives them more opportunity to be spotted by their own particular fan club.

Once you have your core team, you may want to appoint a lead member who is responsible for keeping track of the script and being ready to change the scenery. Alternatively, assign one person to be the lead member for each side of the stage.

Preparing the stage crew to take responsibility for scene changes

Avoid telling the crew immediately what to move and how to move it. Although you probably already have ideas about how the scene changes will run, get the stage crew to try to plan out scene changes for themselves.

The best time to do this is before they actually start working backstage and are still watching from the audience, when you are in the final stages of polishing the show. When they are not on-stage, ask the crew to make up a list of scenes in their running order. Eventually, when they are working backstage, a running list will be posted on either side of the stage, along with a copy of the script for reference.

Ask the stage crew, running list in hand, to sit in the audience, watch the show, and find answers to the following questions:

- Where does the next scene take place?
- If something has to be moved off-stage before the next scene, where will it go? Who should move it?
- If something has to be moved on-stage before the next scene, where is it now? Who should move it?
- Where is the crew member normally before the scene change — for example, exiting stage left? Where is the crew member in his or her next scene — entering stage right for a chorus number?

Ask them to decide who will do what, in what order, and to plan each scene change as best they can. Make sure you coach them how to move objects safely. Once they have done this for a number of scenes, they can start organizing and carrying out the scene changes.

Introducing scene change jargon

Now that your crew has developed some idea what needs to be done, they will find that learning some special stage vocabulary will help them do their tasks properly. They usually enjoy bandying such jargon around. The two basic terms are:

Strike – To remove items from stage

Set – To put items on stage. (Note that items that are moved around the stage between scenes — for example, a desk used in two consecutive scenes — are not "struck." They are simply "re-set" in a different place.)

Other terms they may need to know include:

Blackout – Lights go out completely on-stage while scene change takes place.

Truck – A piece of scenery on wheels.

Lighting cue – A point where there is a change in the lighting.

Sound cue – A point where there is a sound effect or the accompaniment track starts or stops.

The stage crew — including adults and actors — strikes the set.

Top & Tail – To run only the beginnings and ends of scenes, or when special effects happen. This technique is used during scene change rehearsals or technical rehearsals.

The crew may also like to learn some shorthand for some technical terms:

Q – Cue

fx – Effect/effects

Explain to your crew that each scene change is organized into two distinct parts that go one after another:

1. Carry out all the "strikes"
2. Carry out all the "sets"

Instruct them to review the scene changes they have been planning and think about the following:

• Does the scene change follow the strike-set pattern?
• Is there a logical order in setting props where there are several on-stage? For example, what should be put on a table first — the table cloth or the plates? What should go on a bed first — the blankets or the stuffed toys?

Starting to run scene changes

A good time to ask the crew to start changing the scenes is when you begin to run entire scenes back-to-back without stopping the action. This gives the stage crew a realistic idea of how much time they have between each scene change — time they may need to change into a different costume or find some props. Here are some suggestions for these beginning scene changes:

• At the end of a scene, call out "Strike!" Once the correct items have been removed, call out "Set!" These announcements help to create a sense of controlled excitement and urgency.
• At first, the scene will end, you will shout, "Strike," and … absolutely nothing may happen. Simply fetch your crew to the wings and remind them they need to change the scene. As time goes on, their crew work will become part of their individual "show" and you will not have to remind them of what they need to do.
• Once the scene change seems to be running smoothly, note in the script what is being moved and the *character* responsible for moving it. Sketch a diagram of where things need to be on-stage. If your lead stage crew members are up to this, perhaps they can do this for you.

• If some changes are naturally complicated, seem to be taking forever, or are not going as smoothly as you would prefer, make a note to work on them in greater detail during a scene change rehearsal, described in the next section. However, you will find that in many cases the crew has done a logical, creditable job on their own. Congratulate them on what they achieve.

Running a scene change rehearsal

Usually if you try to work out all the light, sound, prop, and scene changes during one huge "technical" rehearsal, it becomes too unwieldy and incredibly long. Consider devoting a session just to rehearse scene changes, so you and the crew can concentrate on polishing and finalizing the scene changes.

In a scene change rehearsal, run the first few lines of each scene. Then cut to the last few lines. The actors rearrange themselves on-stage as they would appear at the end of the scene, with appropriate props having changed hands if required. The actors say or sing the last few lines of the scene. Call out any lighting or sound cues that end the scene, for example, "Blackout!" or "Music plays!"

Run the scene change. Repeat until it appears well choreographed. Finalize any decisions about who strikes or sets the props, which side of the stage they are on, and so on. Record who does what in your master script. If actors are to enter at the end of the scene change, before the next music or light cue, they should do so.

Call out the lighting/sound cues to start the next scene, for example, "Lights up" or "Music." Actors start the next scene and say the first few lines. Cut to the end of the scene and work on the next scene change as before. Continue through the play until all scene changes are finalized and rehearsed.

During the scene change rehearsal, the crew, of course, will be focused on the scene changes. Others not directly involved benefit from thinking about the running order of the show (because each scene is severely shortened), which side of the stage they exit and enter from for each scene, where they need to collect props from, and what costume changes they have. Also explain to the principals that the members of the crew have waited patiently in previous sessions while dialog scenes were rehearsed, and now the principals must wait while the crew rehearses.

The time dedicated to working on scene changes pays off in the performance. Some scene changes, by necessity, are long — or need to be long because of complicated costume changes by the characters. If done before the audience, such scene changes can be a magical transformation of the set from one location to another. Take extra care with these so they look choreographed, evenly paced and stately, and not rushed, noisy, or panicked. Don't let the audience start thinking that the stage crew is struggling or needs help.

Long scene changes that take place behind a closed curtain can be even more challenging to keep under control, but you must persist working with your stage crew so they carry out scene changes smoothly and quietly. There is nothing like the sound of thumps and bumps rising to a crescendo to make the audience wonder, "*What* is going on?" It is far better to make the scene change a few seconds longer — get the pianist to play a rousing reprise of a favorite show tune.

Lifting and handling objects safely

Your stage crew, and in fact, almost everyone in the group and the parents who assist backstage in general, need to know and use safe lifting and moving procedures. You may want to take ten or fifteen minutes and review standard ways of safely lifting and moving bulky items.

General pointers on lifting are as follows:
- If the item seems large, or if you are not sure you can lift it by yourself, always ask an adult to help you. You may need to form a moving team.
- When you do lift an object, even if it seems light, follow these steps:
    1. Stand close to the item, with your feet shoulder-width apart, one foot slightly in front of the other. If the item is on the floor or a low table, bend your knees to reach it, not your back.
    2. Take hold of the item. Use the palms of hands, not just your fingers, to hold it, and try to put your hands under the item, not just on the sides. Keep your elbows close to your body and don't stick them out. Sticking-out elbows look funny, and you can hurt your back.
    3. Use the strength in your legs and thighs, not your back,

to lift the object. As you hold and move the object, keep your back straight. Don't bend it or twist it. If you tuck your chin under a little, you will find it easier to keep your back straight.

4. When you lower an item, keep your chin tucked in and bend your legs, not your back. Try not to drop the object suddenly, you may hurt your fingers and/or break the object. Your back does not have to stay straight up and down, but it has to stay straight.

Making the Transition from Rehearsal to Performance Venue

If you do use separate rehearsal and performance venues, here are some tips for helping the actors make a smooth transition from one to another:

• The first session at the new venue should be an hour longer than usual, which allows the group to become familiar with their new environment before you actually start to work.

• If this is the session where the cast first uses the mikes that come with the venue, allow another extra thirty minutes for learning how to use the mikes.

• Two sessions before you make the move, send home with the participants the list of dates and times you will be in the new venue, along with a map and directions to the venue. Remind them that the first session at the new venue will be longer than usual, and state the exact starting and ending times.

• The session before the move, remind everyone of the new location and ask if there are any problems. Check your attendance record: if someone has missed both sessions, take steps, either by telephone, mail, or through another responsible child, to inform the actor and parents of the new venue, dates and times of the sessions, and directions.

• Before you meet the group at the new venue, sketch out a plan in your mind as to where you will be keeping costumes and props during the show, where the dressing and waiting areas will be and so forth. If it has been months since you reserved it, revisit it.

• When you meet at the new venue, give the group a guided tour of the auditorium area, the stage, and other facilities such as

201

dressing rooms, the greenroom, and restrooms. Things to cover include how to get from one side of the stage to another without actually crossing the on-stage area and where props and costumes will be kept during performances.

- The biggest challenge for the group will be simply to become accustomed to the new stage area, which may be bigger/smaller/darker/lighter than what they have grown used to, and how to get on and off the stage.
- After the tour, put the whole group on the stage and re-teach them stage right and stage left. This may seem like a redundant exercise, but most of them are used to using visual clues to help them distinguish the two; for example, the windows used to be on the right and the clock on the left. In the new venue, there may be no windows and no clock. So you need to remind them of how things used to be: "Right is where the window used to be!" "Left is where the clock used to be."
- Play the Upstage/Downstage game to help them get used to the new space.
- Take them through the big opening number so they start to feel at home in the new space.
- Take them through the beginnings and endings of the rest of the scenes so they become used to where they enter and exit.
- During the first technical and dress rehearsals, do expect some entrances from and exits to the wrong sides of the stage. Simply correct the actors immediately and have them repeat the action in the right direction.

Preparing Actors to Use Props and Costumes

Post the master lists of costumes and properties that you sent home with the kids around the dressing room areas, so they can easily check what they need for which character.

Be aware that when you arrive with new props and costumes to the rehearsals, *all* the group members will want to try on or play with the interesting (or even uninteresting) ones: the fuzzy gray wig, the glittering diamond tiara, the shiny gun, the red squirting carnation. Let them all have a turn and get it out of their systems — but do this in a systematic way.

First, gather the entire group together. Don't show the props and costumes piecemeal to individual actors as they arrive, which results in a Chinese whisper of actors trying to explain things to each other. Show all the props and costumes that have arrived for the first time this rehearsal and demonstrate their correct and *gentle* use before *anyone* is allowed to handle them. Explain that nothing must be broken — replacements, at this point, are hard to find. Then let people take turns with the different props and costumes. The group will be excited and rowdy, but a bit of momentary chaos now will reap the benefits of a calmer, more focused group during the show, when you need calm and they need focus.

Remind each cast member to actually look at, and not merely think about, the list of things they need for the show. Point out the lists you have posted around the dressing room areas and backstage. Do they have their props with them? Do they know where to find them?

Tips for Managing Props and Costumes Backstage

Once your players have had a chance to see what the props can do and try on the costumes, give orders that only the stage crew or the person who brings it/uses it on stage should touch the prop.

Repeat to your performers and any adult helpers that, unless they are a member of the stage crew and have been specifically instructed otherwise, any prop *must* be left in place backstage, never be moved, and not be played with. Try to control yourself when a well-meaning parent comes to you with a basket of flowers and says, "I found this on the floor ..."

Before *each* dress rehearsal and performance, assign a specially designated stage crew member to check that all props and scenery items are in place. Use a master list. As a backup, you should go backstage and have a look yourself and check that all the scenery pieces are intact and that all the props are ready and in place. Things can get a bit sloppy after the excitement of the first performance, and suddenly things aren't in the places they are supposed to be.

If for some reason a prop does disappear, don't waste inordinate amounts of time searching for it. The actors usually aren't thrown by having to mime an object — it's what they have been doing most of the rehearsals anyway.

Directorial Comments During Final Rehearsals

Once you have arrived at the final rehearsals, you will be thinking largely about technical issues and last-minute crises. Hopefully, all the work you and your cast have done over the thirty or so sessions have achieved a rounded, energetic performance that is beginning to take on an exciting life of its own.

Try, if possible, to refrain from any kind of detailed commentary. It's too late for your performers to take much on board. Technical and dress rehearsals are long, and holding everyone for thirty to forty-five minutes afterwards when all they want to do is go home is a pointless exercise.

Starting with the technical rehearsal, always gather everyone together, either in the audience or backstage and give your group a little pep talk before you begin the actual work on-stage. Emphasize the positive things happening in the show, list your Oscar nominations from the previous rehearsal, and present an Oscar to the most deserving cast member. Remind them, and if possible give them examples from their peers' performances, of the need for energy, volume, picking up cues, and smiles.

Of course you can complain about their performance, if you are disappointed. Just be sure to tell them *how*, specifically, they can improve it. For example, you might say, "What happened last night? That final scene just went flat — I thought I was at the dentists' from the gloom coming off the stage! Tonight, I want you all to try think of the silliest joke you have ever heard before you come on-stage, so I can see some energy and *smiles*!"

Always imply that you believe they can do it perfectly. Say things like, "Remember, a few rehearsals ago we learned that if the first couple comes right to the end of downstage right, there is enough room for everyone to line up! Try this again tonight, so I don't have to see everyone falling all over each other."

Give any announcements of technical issues — where props are being stored, and so forth.

This might also be a good time, if you are using rented scripts that need to be returned, to remind everyone they need to be returned.

Chapter 15

The Performances and Beyond

Technical Considerations

No matter how well everything worked at the last rehearsal or performance, it is amazing what can suddenly stop working for no apparent reason. You and your technicians should arrive early enough to test all microphones, cables, lights, musical instruments, and sound equipment. Make a short walk through the stage and backstage areas and check all props and scenery. As your actors arrive, make sure they have brought their own props, if any, and that any special props, such as squirting carnations, are working.

Before each performance, after you give your pep talk to the actors (see below), always take one last walk through the stage and backstage areas and check that all props are in place.

Special notes for the final performance

If you are collecting the costumes, set up pre-labeled bags or boxes, for example "hats," "guns," "Hot Box outfits," "Salvation Army outfits," or "vests. " Line up an adult helper to get the kids to put each costume article into the correct bag at the end of the show. This will save you from having to sort them out later, and from having fifty people ask you, "Where should I put this?" You simply have to point.

If you need to dismantle and pack away the set for moving, try to arrange for this to happen immediately after the last performance. You will have lots of people around at this time, and most will be willing to lend a hand. Make sure you have all the tools necessary for the task and enough of them so no one has to stand around waiting for something to do. There's nothing like trying to find ten screwdrivers at 10:00 P.M. on a Saturday night.

Be sure someone is available to collect any rented scripts if you have been using them.

Front-of-House Duties

For performances, you will need help with "Front-of-house" duties, or those tasks carried out for the benefit of the audience attending the show. These include selling and collecting tickets, ushering the audience to reserved seats if used, handing out programs, and selling refreshments. In some cases, you may need help to set out the chairs before each performance, put them away afterwards, and tidy up the building. See the section "Recruiting Extra Help for the Final Rehearsals and Performances," in chapter 14 for details of these roles and the tasks involved.

At the same time, your cast can help in some ways. They can help set up chairs on arrival if your venue requires it, and help put them away after the show. Be sure they understand any duties they may be expected to carry out. Explain them to your group at the final dress rehearsal.

Talking to the Actors before the Show

Each night of the performance, as with the dress rehearsals, you should gather your cast together about five minutes before the show starts and give them a little pep talk. The content will vary slightly depending on which night of performance you are presenting.

Opening night

The actors will be extremely nervous and excited. Don't spend a lot of time trying to keep them quiet, even if the walls between the waiting area and the audience may be thin. They may be worried that something will go wrong and they won't be able to cope. The following are some suggestions on what to cover during this talk:

- Remind them how hard they have been working and that they have a show to be proud of. Tell them whatever happens, keep going!
- They need to be loud when they speak and they need to sing out when they sing. If the audience is filling up, tell them so and remind them to project so those in the back can hear. If the audience is small, don't admit it. Just say, "We have a good audience tonight — make sure you are loud enough so everyone can easily hear."

• A useful admonition is, "Eyes and teeth!" Keep on a big smile during big numbers, keep a bright face out to the audience, and imagine your eyes are sparkling like diamonds. This gives them something to concentrate on, calms nerves, and makes them more easily seen.

• Remind them of anything that might affect their safety — jumping on and off platforms, watching microphone cables.

• Remind them of any technical things, perhaps prefacing your comment with "Remember, we learned at dress rehearsal ... you need to stay in the light and not move too far downstage" or "the platforms take up a lot of room so don't crowd each other in front of them, try to space yourselves out a bit more to either side."

• Remind them about any after-show tasks, such as gathering up all their costumes and taking them home or hanging them up, or stacking chairs in the audience area. Start reminding them which costumes they can keep after the show, and which they are to return. Plan to collect any costumes you want returned on the last night of the performance before they go home, never to be seen again. Remind them to check in any rented scripts if they are ready to return them.

• Introduce your adult helpers/backstage monitors. Remind your cast that these adults have authority over them.

• Give out the Oscar from the last rehearsal. Wish everyone a wonderful performance.

"Middle" performances

You may find your actors' levels of excitement and nervousness dip for the second performance — and any other performance — until the final night. They may also be a bit tired, having undergone a few nights of long dress rehearsals and the excitement of opening night.

In your pep talk for these performances, you need to pump up your actors and make sure they maintain the energy and pace necessary to engage their audience. In these talks, concentrate on the following:

• The audience, barring a few parents, has never seen the show before, so the actors still need to be loud, strong, and show plenty "eyes and teeth." Tell them, no matter how filled the theatre actually is, that they have a great audience, and that you expect they will give the best show possible.

- Any safety/technical reminders.
- After-show duties. Remind them which costumes they can keep and which need to be returned, preferably the last night of the show.
- Mention any nominations for Oscars from the previous performance and the reasons for them, making sure they are usually connected to energy levels. Then present the Oscar for the previous evening and remind everyone you are looking for the winner of the next one to have the most energetic, focused performance of the cast. This usually incites interest to produce the best possible show.

Final performance

You will find your cast has regained a lot of the excitement, but not the nerves, of opening night. Therefore, you need to guard against their putting on a sloppy show. Focus on the following:

- This will be the last time before an audience, so they need to make the most of it and present a truly remarkable, energetic, and well paced show. They need to give the show everything they've got.
- Safety/technical reminders
- After-show duties — which may be more involved on the last night. Remind them which costumes they can keep and which need to be returned, preferably immediately after the show that evening.
- Oscar presentations. Remind them that you are still looking for one more, which will be given at the final workshop session or immediately after the show if no workshops are scheduled to take place after the show.

During the Performances

During the performances, you need to watch the show; don't retire to the dressing room where you can only get bits and pieces of the performance. Staying backstage, you will be bombarded with trivial matters, for example, "Where's my hat?" or "Can I have a Coke?" or "Do I have time to go to the bathroom?" Your backstage monitors will handle any issues backstage — and if a true emergency arises, you will know about it.

You should not have any technical duties, such as lighting or sound. All these tasks should have been delegated to your adult helpers. However, if your lighting person suddenly phones in sick, you will at least be there to fill those particular shoes. You are the free-floating troubleshooter.

If you have been working with a very experienced and mature set of actors, you can sit in the back row, relax, and watch the show. However, the reality is that young performers still need you! You need to sit down front center, where you can see the show, *and they can see you.* From this vantage point, you can:

- Help them remember the dance routines by miming the motions.
- Indicate where they need to start singing after a musical bridge.
- Motion as to whether they need to be louder or softer in singing volume.
- Gesture to the chorus lurking uncertainly off-stage that, yes, they need to come on *now.*
- Pull in an actor whose attention has gone off on a "Sunday stroll."
- Keep their confidence high that things are going well. Keep smiling and nodding energetically and you will be rewarded with a more energetic performance.
- See and, if possible, correct any technical problems. For example, if a mike goes down, direct the actor to a working one. If worse come to worst, you can quietly leave and find the crucial prop you realize has not been set and surreptitiously get it on-stage.

After the Show Ends Each Night

Your actors may have a school day the following morning, so don't expect them to meet with you as a group after the show. They will go to see any family or friends who have come to the show, and then disappear very quickly. Be on hand to remind them to gather costumes, put away chairs and anything else you have told them they are expected to do. Organize adult helpers as quickly as possible to complete any tasks.

The final night of the show may require additional tasks, such as dismantling and carting away the set. Again, organize your adult helpers as quickly as possible and make sure they have the right tools for the job.

Be sure to collect any cash from ticket or refreshment sales and stow it securely away. Hopefully, whoever has been ticket secretary for the night will not announce for all to hear, "There's five hundred dollars in here!"

Speaking to the Audience after the Final Performance

Some amateur groups feel it necessary that the director go up on-stage at the end of the final show and make a "thank you" speech. We advise against this. Any thank you's should have already been put into the program or made personally to the helpers. You are likely not to mention everyone who thinks they should be mentioned and you will now have an offended parent or cast member. Your show has spoken for all the efforts you and others have made at any time, and the applause is the true thank you.

However, some groups make it a practice to bring the director, particularly if they are female, on-stage and present them with a bouquet. In this case, you will have no choice but to say something. If you are dragged up in this way, make your acceptance speech short, and avoid getting into a string of thank you's, for the reasons given above. Simply say how much you have enjoyed working on the show and say thanks for the gift. If you have, in fact, decided on the next show, this is an excellent time to announce it. Your last words should throw the limelight back onto the cast. They are the stars; it's their show, their moment, and you cannot repeat that sentiment too many times.

A Final Workshop after the Show

If your schedule permits it, a final workshop after the show will help tie up any loose ends and give a sense of completion to the season's activities. If you need to collect scripts and costumes, here is a final opportunity. However, we find the safest option is to collect as much as you can on the last night of the show.

The following are some activities you might want to include in the last session:

- Hand out letters to bring home regarding when the next season starts, fees, and the name of the next show if known. In the letter, thank all those who helped once again and reiterate how much you enjoyed working with the group.
- Make it a party. It takes some organization and coordination with the parents, but each child can bring some refreshments to share.
- Give the Oscar for the best performance the last night of the show and an Oscar for the best performer over all.
- If you had a competition for ticket sales that included tickets sold at the door, announce the winner and give out the prize.
- Do the opening number one last time. Your group may want to carry on and do most of the show. If so, allow them to do so. If interest seems to flounder, ask them to do some more of the big numbers.
- Divide into groups and prepare scenes from the show for presentation. The actors can swap roles and perhaps wind up with a silly version, where characters play against type.
- Play some theatre games or other games. See chapter 5 or appendix 3 for suggestions. Also, the actors will usually have some ideas of some playground games.
- If you have the next show picked out, present an overview of the action and play some of the songs.

Top Ten Tips for Working with Young Performers

1. **In order to get the actors' attention, clap out a rhythm and program them to copy you whenever they see you do it.** For example, clap your hands and click your fingers to the count of 1-2, 1-2-3 where 1-2 is two slow claps and 1-2-3 is three quick clicks. You can also tap on parts of your body — for example, one finger click, then two taps on a shoulder. Wait until everyone in the room has noticed you and is copying, the last person is usually suitably embarrassed. Finally, change the rhythm to hold their attention and calm them down before you speak.

2. **Don't yell over the top of the actors' noise if you need to speak to them or give instructions.** The louder you are, the noisier they become and they won't be listening anyway. Get them to stop what they are doing and listen properly. When you do speak, vary your volume. If you speak quietly, they will have to listen harder. Again, if you speak in a loud excited tone, they will become louder and more excited.

3. **If the actors start to chatter while you are still speaking, don't waste your energy telling them off;** simply stand silently and stare in their direction. The rest of the group will do the same. The culprits will soon feel all eyes on them and will fall into sheepish silence. Every time someone interrupts you, stop and wait for silence. Don't lose your nerve doing this. It may take ten minutes, but they'll get the message.

4. **Don't wait until all the actors assemble themselves when starting a musical number.** Announce which number you are doing, and ask the cast to take their places. As soon as some of them are there and the music is ready, just *go*. The rest will soon join in and catch up. This strategy saves you going through all the tips listed above only to then tell them during the song, "Be louder!"

5. **When printing or photocopying, mark up the master fully before making copies.** This way you avoid having to make fifty amendments by hand afterwards. For example, if you are using lyric sheets, number them or mark in who is singing certain verses *before* copying the set.

6. **Make the auditions into fun workshops.** Give everyone a chance to try out for all the big parts.

7. **Appoint a lead singer for all chorus numbers.** Lead singers — who may or may not do the routine — should be positioned downstage left and right. Their goal is to keep singing — loudly — when everyone else has stopped because they're concentrating on the steps.

8. **Use the actors as stage crew.** This creates yet more parts for the cast members who may be chorus members or have other small roles. It also avoids the stress of trying to find a group of parents willing to come to several rehearsals, all the performances, and miss watching the actual show on the night they had bought a ticket for. It is also visually more pleasing for the audience if the crew is in costume and in character.

9. **On the last night, label all bags and boxes in which costumes and props are going to be collected.** For example, "hats," "black jackets," "wooden bowls and spoons." This stops everyone from asking you, "Where should I put this?" and it means that items are sorted, ready for storage.

10. **Performance energy is the most valuable commodity on-stage.** Energy communicates itself from one actor to another and then to the audience. Energy is needed in the quietest moments as well as in the most robust musical numbers. It shows conviction and demands attention, and it comes from the actors being totally attentive to what is going on on-stage. Energy captivates the audience so they leave wanting more.

213

Appendix 1

Glossary of Theatrical and Musical Terms

Many websites offer extensive glossaries of theatrical, literary, and musical terms. These sites vary widely in their breadth, technicality, and precision, so look at several definitions — some make more sense or are simpler than others. Dictionaries are also an excellent source of general definitions.

Apron – In a proscenium stage, the portion of the stage that extends toward the audience in front of the front curtain

A-frame set piece – A set piece that can be used on both sides. It stands like an A-frame, often on a moving platform.

Audition – A tryout for a part in a show

Backdrop or backcloth – A large curtain, usually painted to depict a scene, hung at the back of the stage. It can also be undecorated, with lights used to make patterns.

Bar – 1) A short section of music; also the line of music itself. (Also see figure 22 following the glossary) 2) a horizontal metal rod over the stage from which lanterns or backdrops can be hung.

Base clef – (See figure 22 following the glossary)

Blocking – Planned movement on-stage, for example, an actor moves across the stage and sits down

Book flat – A self-supporting hinged flat, usually painted on both sides so it can be used as two different settings

Bridge – A piece of music that fills a gap between action or songs

Cast – The actors who play the characters in a particular show

Chord – More than one note (usually three) played at the same time

Choreography – Planned dance movements; the planning and directing of dance movements

Choreographer – A person who plans and directs the dances of a show

Chorus – Members of the cast who sing, usually in unison, to a song. They often do not have named roles. It also refers to the same set of lines that are sung several times in a song, or the refrain.

Cue – A signal for an actor to say or do something; a signal for some technical or musical effect. It might be a spoken line, a technical effect, or a movement. "Picking up cues" is an important element for a successful show.

Director – The person ultimately responsible for the decisions affecting all elements of a show — acting, technical, musical, and dance

Downstage – Toward the audience

Flat – A unit of stage scenery. It usually consists of a wooden frame covered with muslin and painted.

Fresnel – A stage light used for general, diffused lighting

Front of house – Activities directly involving the audience, such as selling tickets and refreshments, distributing programs, and in general making sure the audience is comfortable

Gobo – A lighting accessory, usually a thin piece of metal that is cut into patterns such as leaves or arcs and placed over a focused light (leko) to produce shadows that give the effect of scenery

Greenroom – A room where performers can relax before or after appearances

Improv(isation) – To make up a scene as the actors go along, without set scripts or lines

Lead – A principal part in a show; important to the plot and action of the story

Leko – A stage light capable of providing a sharply defined light

Libretto – The book containing the sung and spoken words of a musical; the script

Lyrics – The words of a song

Mime – To perform an action without speaking and usually without props

215

Musical director – The person with overall responsibility for directing the singers and musicians in a show

Octave – Any interval of eight consecutive notes on the scale; a note that is eight full notes above or below another

Overture – Instrumental music played before the show begins. It often includes tunes from several songs in the show.

Pantomime – (See mime) This word also refers to the entire presentation of actions performed without words and props.

Principal – A main role in a show, who is important to the plot and action of the story

Prompt – Someone who follows the script and reads the first part of any lines an actor forgets so the actor will be able to complete the rest of the speech by him- or herself.

Prop/Property – Any item used on-stage. Sometimes *rehearsal props* — less expensive or less realistic items — are used in rehearsals before the dress rehearsals.

Proscenium – A kind of theatre where the audience sits and watches the action through a "frame," which is the proscenium.

Refrain – The same set of lines that are repeated several times during a song

Rostrums – Moveable platforms that can be used on-stage for different purposes.

Score – A set of written musical notes. A full score will show notes for all parts — vocal and instrumental — whereas a vocal score will have only the notes of the singer or singers. Also refers to the action of writing or rearranging music.

Script – All the spoken lines and sung words of a play, together with any written stage directions.

Set – 1) The physical representation of a setting. If the setting is a palace, the set might be a backdrop and throne. 2) To put an item on the stage during a scene change.

Setting – Where the action takes place

Staff/Staves – The five lines used in musical notation. (See figure 22 following the glossary)

Stanza – A group of lyrics of a song that have the same or a very similar pattern or rhyme and rhythm.

Strike – To remove an item from the stage during a scene change.

Treble clef – (See figure 22 following the glossary)

Upstage – 1) Away from the audience 2) To block or draw attention away from the most important actor or action

Vamp – To play a bar or bars of music repeatedly to cover a scene change or actors coming onto the stage

Verse – (See stanza)

Wings – Off-stage areas to the left and right of a proscenium stage

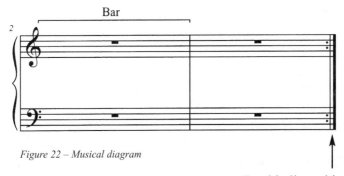

Figure 22 – Musical diagram

Double line with dots means repeat last set of bars, beginning at the first double line with dots.

Appendix 2
Resources

The Internet or your local community or college library can provide a wealth of possible resources or ways to get them. The lists provided here are just a start.

Scripts
The rights to musicals seem to change hands on a regular basis. A useful website is http://www.musicals101.com, which includes a regularly updated list of musicals and their rights owners.

Royalty musicals
U.S.
Contemporary Drama Service
885 Elkton Drive
Colorado Springs, Colorado 80907
Tel: 719-594-4422
Order Line (toll-free within North America): 800-937-5297
Fax: 719-594-9916
Email: MerPCDS@aol.com
www.contemporarydrama.com

Dramatists Play Service, Inc.
440 Park Avenue South
New York, New York 10016
Tel: 212-683-8960
Fax: 212-213-1539
Email: postmaster@dramatists.com
www.dramatists.com

Music Theatre International (MTI)
421 West 54th Street
New York, New York 10019
Tel: 212-541-4684
Fax: 212-397-4684
Email: Licensing@MTIshows.com
www.mtishows.com

Pioneer Drama Service, Inc.
PO Box 4267
Englewood, Colorado 80155-4267
Tel: 303-779-4035
Toll free: 800-333-7262
Fax: 303-779-4315
Email: orders@pioneerdrama.com
www.pioneerdrama.com

Samuel French, Inc.
45 West 25th Street – Dept.W
New York, New York 10010
Tel: 212-206-8990
Fax: 212-206-1429

Canada
Samuel French (Canada) Ltd.
100 Lombard Street – Dept.W
Toronto, Ontario M5C 1M3
Tel: 416-363-3536
Fax: 416-363-1108
http://www.samuelfrench.com/

U.K.

A useful website is "The Guide to Musical Theatre," (www.nodanw.com) which provides information regarding performance rights to both songs and plays, and provides a comprehensive list of license holders.

Josef Weinberger Ltd.
12-14 Mortimer Street
London W1T 3JJ
Tel: 020 7580 2827
Fax: 020 7436 9616
Email: general.info@jwmail.co.uk
www.josef-weinberger.co.uk
This company provides junior and school versions of musicals for groups in the UK and Ireland. Email address for information regarding junior/school versions and showkits: amateur@jwmail.co.uk

MusicScope
95 White Lion Street
London N1 9PF
Tel: 020 7278 1133
Fax: 020 7278 4442
MusicScope controls the rights in the U.K. to a number of plays and musicals that are available in the U.S. from other companies.

Samuel French Ltd.
52 Fitzroy Street
London W1T 5JR
Tel: 020 7387 9373
Fax: 020 7387 2161
www.samuelfrench-london.co.uk

Chappells
Shows controlled by this license holder are now obtainable through Josef Weinberger Ltd. in London.

Other international
If you are working with a group elsewhere, check the websites of the companies listed below to obtain information about the office nearest you.

Dance Notation
Dance Notation Bureau, http://dancenotation.org/DNB/
Iver Cooper's Action Stroke Dance Notation,
http://www.geocities.com/Broadway/Stage/2806/
The Center For Sutton Movement Writing, Inc.
P.O. Box 517
La Jolla, California 92038-0517
USA
Tel: 858-456-0098
Fax: 858-456-0020
www.dancewriting.org

Criminal Records Bureau (CRB) Disclosure (U.K.: England and Wales)
To apply for Criminal Records Bureau (CRB) disclosure, contact the CRB (Disclosure).
Mailing address:
P.O. Box 110
Liverpool L3 6ZZ
Information line: 0870 909 0811
http://www.disclosure.gov.uk

Resources for Learning Skills of Stage, Dance and Musical Direction, Stagecraft
Meriwether Publishing Ltd. offers a wide selection of books with practical, low-cost ideas for sets, costumes, and makeup. It also has a number of books on stage and theatre directing.
Meriwether Publishing Ltd.
885 Elkton Drive
Colorado Springs, CO 80907
Tel: 719-594-4422
Email: MerPCDS@aol.com
www.meriwether.com

For dance and music direction, you need to understand these arts from a performance level. You also need some music theory. Sign up for classes or other instructional opportunities available in your local community!

Insurance
U.K.

If you do not have the required insurance to perform for the public, insurance can be arranged with First Act Insurance.

First Act Insurance
Simpson House
6 Cherry Orchard Road
Croydon, CR9 5BB
England
Tel: 020 8686 5050
Fax: 020 8686 5559
http://www.firstact.co.uk

Costume Rental
Using the Internet

For Internet searches in the U.K., try "fancy dress hire," "costume hire" or "historical costume hire," followed by either "U.K." or the town in which you are located if you want a more local supplier. Use similar key words if you use www.yell.co.uk.

For Internet searches in the U.S., try "costume rental" or "historical costume rental" followed by "U.S." or the town in which you are located if you want a more local supplier. Use the same key words if you employ www.yell.com.

U.S.

Ivywild Costumes
1616 S. Tejon St.
Colorado Springs, CO 80906
Tel: 719-633-9129
Toll free: 800-950-9129
Fax: 719-633-9016
Email: lindrama@aol.com
http://www.ivywildcostumes.com

U.K. companies
Midland Costume Ltd.
Theatre Court
Derrington Avenue
Crewe
Cheshire CW2 7JB
Tel: 01270 251288
Fax: 01270 251289

The Pantomime Shop
Units 2 and 3
Heaton Street Mill
Heaton Street
Denton
Manchester M34 3RG
Tel: 0161 320 4345

Flame Torbay Costume Hire Ltd.
31-35 Market Street
Torquay TQ1 3AW
www.flametorbay.co.uk
Tel: 01803 211930
Fax: 01803 293554

W.A. Homburg Ltd.
King House
17 Regent Street
Leeds LS2 7UZ
Tel: 0113 245 8425
Fax: 0113 243 0635
Email: hire@homburgs.co.uk
www.homburgs.co.uk

Scenery, Property, and Lighting Equipment Purchase, Rental, or Hire

U.K.

If you search on the Internet, use "stage scenery hire" as key words. There are many suppliers; finding one close to you will help decrease shipping costs.

Howorth Wrightson Ltd.
Unit 2, Cricket St.
Denton
Manchester M34 3DR
Tel: 0161 335 0220
Fax: 0161 320 3928
Email: props@hwltd.co.uk
www.hwltd.co.uk

The Border Studio
Riverside Mill
Level Crossing
Selkirk
TD7 5EQ
Tel: 01750 20237
Fax: 01750 20313
Email: info@borderstudio.com
http://www.borderstudio.com/home.html

U.S.

If you search on the Internet, use "theatrical scenery rental" as key words.

Weber-Prianti Scenic Studio
408 A. Meco Drive
Wilmington, DE 19804
Tel: 302-998-7567
Toll-Free: 888-997-5600
Fax: 302-998-6931
Email: info@wpscenic.com
http://www.backdropsonline.com/

Utah Shakesperean Festival
315 W. Center Street
Cedar City, UT 84720
Tel: 435-586-7779
http://services.bard.org/

Fullerton Civic Light Opera Co. (Rental Division)
218 W. Commonwealth
Fullerton, CA 92832
Scenic Rental and Properties: 714-992-0710
Costume Rental: 714-879-9761
Email: Rentfclo@aol.com
http://www.fclo.com/

Appendix 3

Games to Develop Acting Skills

Stage Terms

Use the same idea as Upstage/Downstage (explained in chapter 5) but ask the performers to mime different theatrical tasks, using appropriate terminology. As with the earlier game, the last one to begin the mime is "out," but can then help by writing down ideas of different actions, or helping you decide who is the last one.

Examples:

- Rig the lighting – mime climbing a ladder or attaching lights to a batten
- Put your makeup on – mime applying makeup
- Fly the scenery – mime pulling down on a rope to raise a backcloth
- Open the house tabs – mime winding a large handle or pulley to open the front curtains
- Quick change – mime changing costumes very quickly
- Follow spot – mime following an actor across a stage with a large spotlight
- Run a flat – mime running across the stage with a large flat piece of scenery
- Set up for act 1 – mime bringing furniture/scenery on for the opening
- Strike the set – mime taking furniture/scenery off

Memory, Listening, and Voice Projection (Silly Outside Summer Game)

The group members have so much fun with this that they really don't think that they are working and often go home saying, "We just played games."

This game is to be played outside on hot summer days — everyone gets wet!

Directions:

1. Everyone sits in a circle. They are each an actor in a "cast."
2. Someone is chosen to be the first "Agent."
3. The Agent stands in the middle and writes on a piece of paper the name of one of the actors in the circle.
4. The paper is folded and given to the group leader so no one can peek.
5. The group leader hands the Agent a plastic vessel with two to three cm of water in it.
6. The Agent walks around the inside of the circle in a clockwise direction and asks each actor in turn to name another actor in the "cast."
7. When someone says the name of the actor the Agent wrote on the paper, the Agent throws the water at the person who said it. A good rule is to say the water must be thrown below the neck. A bit of a chase may ensue.
8. The Agent returns to the circle as an actor. The person on his or her left becomes the next Agent and so the game proceeds with everyone getting a turn.
9. After writing a name on the paper, the new Agent starts with the actor to the left of the person who got wet so that you are not always going back to the same starting point.
10. No names are allowed to be repeated; this forces the group to pay attention to listening and memory skills.
11. Everyone has to speak loudly and clearly because the Agent is inside the circle — hence the need for voice projection.

Obviously you have to use your common sense concerning the water throwing. Decide if it is warm enough to be playing the game and whether or not the parents will mind. If you decide against the water, one variation is for the Agent to chase and tag the named actor.

Variations:

You can use a whole variety of categories of items instead of the actors' names.

The Agent writes an item on the piece of paper, and then the people in the circle start listing possibilities. When the correct item is named, that person gets wet.

Examples include:

• The names of characters in the show
• Names of props in the show
• Things to do with holidays — either summer vacation time or the current public holiday or religious event.
• Theatrical terminology

Try to choose something finite or the game could last all day.

About the Authors

Adele Firth (neé Lawson) grew up in Manchester, England. She studied drama at Mountview Theatre School, London, and spent six years working as an actress in repertory theatre. She went on to train as a primary school teacher. She now works in various schools in South Manchester and runs three branches of Adele Lawson's School of Theatre for actors aged six to sixteen. She happily became Mrs. Firth when she married Peter in June 2002.

Maria Novelly grew up in Oklahoma and Texas. She studied English and drama at Colorado College, Colorado Springs, and the University of Texas, Austin. She went on to teach English and drama at schools in Texas and Ramstein Air Base, Germany. She now resides with her husband and children in Stockport, England, which is just outside of Manchester. She met Adele when her son Matt attended the Adele Lawson School of Theatre Saturday workshops for four years and both she and her son became involved in the shows. This book is a result of trying to distill Adele's ability to take thirty kids and put on a full-length musical that builds the performers' skills and confidence and gives the audience a gift of genuine enjoyment.

Order Form

TM

Meriwether Publishing Ltd.
PO Box 7710
Colorado Springs CO 80933-7710
Phone: 800-937-5297 Fax: 719-594-9916
Website: www.meriwether.com

Please send me the following books:

_____ **Staging Musicals for Young Performers**   **$19.95**
#BK-B271
by Maria C. Novelly and Adele Firth
How to produce a show in 36 sessions or less

_____ **Theatre Games for Young Performers**   **$16.95**
#BK-B188
by Maria C. Novelly
Improvisations and exercises for developing acting skills

_____ **More Theatre Games for Young Performers** **$17.95**
#BK-B268
by Suzi Zimmerman
Improvisations and exercises for developing acting skills

_____ **Elegantly Frugal Costumes #BK-B125**   **$15.95**
by Shirley Dearing
A do-it-yourself costume maker's guide

_____ **Stagecraft I #BK-B116**   **$19.95**
by William H. Lord
A complete guide to backstage work

_____ **Acting Games — Improvisations and**   **$16.95**
Exercises #BK-B168
by Marsh Cassady
A textbook of theatre games and improvisations

_____ **Audition Monologs for Student Actors**   **$15.95**
#BK-B232
edited by Roger Ellis
Selections from contemporary plays

These and other fine Meriwether Publishing books are available at
your local bookstore or direct from the publisher. Prices subject to
change without notice. Check our website or call for current prices.

Name: _____ e-mail: _____

Organization name: _____

Address: _____

City: _____ State: _____

Zip: _____ Phone: _____
   ❏ **Check enclosed**
   ❏ **Visa / MasterCard / Discover #** _____
                                        Expiration
Signature: _____ *date:* _____
        (required for credit card orders)

Colorado residents: Please add 3% sales tax.
Shipping: Include $3.95 for the first book and 75¢ for each additional book ordered.

   ❏ *Please send me a copy of your complete catalog of books and plays.*